Field Guide to the Flora of
GROOTBOS NATURE RESERVE

and the Walker Bay region

SEAN PRIVETT & HEINER LUTZEYER

Author: Sean Privett
Photographer: Heiner Lutzeyer
Additional photography by: Martin Mergili (pp 41, 42), Michael Langford (p 49), Juan Moreiras (pp 12, 127 'Sugarbird on Protea' & back cover 'Sugarbird on Protea'), Obie Oberholzer (pp 6, 15, 16, 19) and Karen Schermbrucker (p 21)
Cover photo: Martin Kirchner
Colour retouching: Ikhala Graphic Communications
Concept and design: Patricia Lynch-Blom (patz@zeplins.com)
Project manager: Andy Wonnacott
Proofreaders: Lily Upton, Cynthia Privett, Lindsay Norman
Printed and bound by: Craft Print International Ltd, Singapore

ISBN number. 978-0-620-47805-2

First published in 2010 by the Grootbos Foundation

Website: www.grootbos.com

This book contains general information about medicinal plants and their uses. It is intended as an overview and not as a medicinal handbook for self-treatment. Do not attempt self-diagnosis or self-treatment. Always consult a medicinal professional or qualified practitioner. The authors cannot be held responsible for claims arising from the use of these plants.

☆☆☆☆☆

GROOTBOS FOUNDATION

The proceeds from the sale of this book go to the Grootbos Foundation.

The Grootbos Foundation is a registered section 21, non-profit company that is audited annually by KPMG. The Foundation is funded through its own Green Futures nursery and landscaping business, through sale of products from the Growing the Future food production project, support from Grootbos as well as other corporate and individual sponsors. Support can be for a specific project such as towards a bursary for a Green Futures or Growing the Future student, planting a Future Tree or sponsoring sports equipment or coaches for the Football Foundation programme. Alternatively, donations can be a more general contribution towards the work of the Foundation.

For more information on our current needs, contact info@greenfutures.co.za, or take a look at our website www.grootbosfoundation.org.za

Bank details: Grootbos Green Futures Foundation
First National Bank, Hermanus Branch
Branch code: 200412
Current Account number: 62064420856
Swift Code: FIRNZAJJ
The Grootbos Foundation is a registered Public Benefit Organisation (PBO number 930023319).

CONTENTS

FOREWORD

Humanity has had a long relationship with the Cape's seductive flora, from its initial importance as a source of food and medicine to the subcontinent's first inhabitants, passing through its roles in the expanding science of plant taxonomy and horticulture, to our current appreciation of its fragililty and uncertain future. The formal study of South African wildflowers dates from the end of the sixteenth century, when a dried flower head of *Protea neriifolia* reached Holland in 1597, perplexing the botanical fraternity by its strangeness. Flowering bulbs soon followed, their brilliant blooms igniting a passion for the Cape flora that reached its apogee at the turn of the eighteenth century, a period dubbed the *Kaapzeit*, when exotic novelties from the Cape bolstered the reputations of the rich and royal throughout Europe. Private and commercial collectors flocked to the subcontinent in search of rarities to adorn the herbaria and botanical gardens of all Europe.

Our knowledge of the Cape flora has increased tremendously since these early years but such is the richness of the Cape that the discovery of unnamed species remains a reality. The past decade alone has seen the publication of over 300 newly named wildflower species from the region. For long treated as one of the six Floristic Kingdoms of the world, the Cape flora has recently assumed a more modest but no less distinctive rank within the flora of sub-Saharan Africa. A little under 91 000 km² in extent, the Cape Floristic Region encompasses 9 250 known species of flowering plants, making it one of the most diverse floras in the world. Well over two thirds of these species do not extend beyond its boundaries, with the majority restricted to very small portions within it, sometimes to a single mountainside or valley bottom. It is this characteristic that makes the discovery of new species a real possibility, even in relatively well populated areas.

Intensive exploration of Grootbos Nature Reserve, under the initiative of Heiner Lutzeyer and Sean Privett, has produced an impressive checklist of 765 vascular plants, including six newly described species, of which four are still known only from the reserve. In an age when the unknown is now a rare commodity, the Cape still provides rich opportunities for discovery. In a salutary lesson, Sean and Heiner have demonstrated that the majority of the rarest and most endangered species are discovered only after several years' intensive collecting, highlighting the very real problem that superficial surveys of biodiversity are predestined to overlook the very species that they are supposed to protect! The value of these findings, however, depends on their implementation, and the true impact of Grootbos may well be in its extended outreach and community projects.

Respect and appreciation of the environment are all too readily dismissed as elitist affectations, whereas they underpin our psychical and physical wellbeing. One third of all Cape plant species endure some level of threat and almost one fifth face extinction, primarily from agriculture and urban and coastal development. The only way that we can prevent a large portion of our much loved but chronically neglected Cape flora from passing into history is to set aside areas for its survival. Grootbos and similar private reserves show what can be achieved through dedication and commitment, and we are well advised to follow their example.

DR JOHN MANNING
South African National
Biodiversity Institute

In May 1991, when we first came to Grootbos, the incredible view of Walker Bay to the distant Cape of Good Hope overwhelmed me from the first second I stood on our potential property. The stunning natural surroundings with blossoms shining in their most brilliant colours, green fynbos bushes and old Milkwood trees gave me the feeling that here I was part of paradise. It was only when fynbos enthusiast Sean Privett joined the Grootbos team in 1997 to become our first fynbos guide and conservation manager that I truly realised what I had growing right outside my front door. Sean opened our eyes to the diversity and uniqueness of fynbos as well as the complex symbiotic relationships between plants, insects and animals that also made our farm their home. From the very beginning our vision was to create something unique out of what we had, even if the beginnings were a little bit humble. Hard work, enthusiasm, honesty, support by friends, investors and staff and strong family co-operation was the recipe for the success of Grootbos. My father Heiner invested his money in the original purchase of Grootbos, but far more significantly he has invested much of his retirement in methodically photographing and identifying the Grootbos flora. I could never have imagined that the farm we bought back in 1991, together with the neighbouring properties that we have purchased over the years that followed would be home to over 760 species of plants, including six that are totally new to science.

While I am extremely proud of the world-class tourism business we have developed at Grootbos, I am even more proud of our achievements in conservation and community upliftment. We have always been innovative and have been inspired to contribute to South Africa's future in terms of developing knowledge and skills amongst all South Africans. I have no doubt that this guide to the flora of Grootbos and Walker Bay will provide an important tool in informing and inspiring people to conserve our unique natural heritage.

It has been a long walk to make Grootbos what it is today, and our journey is far from over. Call it luck or destiny, but it all comes from that unique view, remarkable natural assets and a dream to create something valuable out of apparently nothing – and in our case dreams sometimes do come true!

MICHAEL LUTZEYER
Founder and Managing Director
Grootbos Nature Reserve

5

ACKNOWLEDGEMENTS

This book is the result of 13 years of botanical research on Grootbos, beginning in 1997 with the initial survey undertaken by Sean Privett and Graeme Siebrits. It was at this early stage that we first received invaluable support with plant identification by the team at the Compton Herbarium in Kirstenbosch. Over the years we have made countless visits to the herbarium where the staff have gone out of their way to assist us in identifying even the most dreadful 'eco-scraps' of plant material. We would especially like to thank John Manning for always making time to welcome us to his office and assist in identifying our plants. John also assisted us greatly with this book in providing input on nomenclature and ordering of species and checking final layout and names. We also wish to acknowledge the friendly assistance of Edwina Marinus, Koos Roux, Ted Oliver, Dee Snijman, Anthony Magee, Chris Cupido, Graham Duncan, Hubert Kurzweil, Cornelia Klak and Terry Trinder-Smith (Bolus Herbarium). We thank Professor Richard Cowling for his mentorship, support and encouragement over the years. The book would not have been possible without the financial assistance of Frank and Lizelle Kilbourn and the Bright Foundation for which we are extremely grateful. It was brought to fruition by Andy Wonnacott of Electric Storm and Patricia Lynch-Blom of Bookart. Finally, without Michael, Dorothee, Tertius and Gabi Lutzeyer's vision and unerring determination to make Grootbos what it is today, we would be no further in understanding the remarkable diversity and conservation value of the flora of the Walker Bay region of the Cape.

Until recently, few people, if any, would have guessed the rich extent of the species of plants found in the Walker Bay area, and Grootbos in particular. With the publication of this book, which was built on the passion and conservation ethos of Sean Privett and the Lutzeyer family, all of us can now marvel at the incredible diversity found in this beautifully preserved area.

The Bright Foundation is privileged to be involved in and associated with the conservation projects at Grootbos. In supporting the publication of thirteen years of dedicated research and documentation, the Foundation achieves two of its main objectives, namely conservation and education.

We, as founders and trustees of the Bright Foundation, share in the joy of this achievement. Our hope is that this project will convince all Grootbos' neighbours to dedicate more and more land to the conservation of fynbos and encourage further research into sustainable farming and tourism practices in this beautiful area.

May we all learn from Heiner Lutzeyer, that its never too late to start anew, to look afresh, at the bounty around us.

FRANK AND LIZELLE KILBOURN

ANTON AND ELPHI TALJAARD

Grootbos, August 2010

BRIGHT
FOUNDATION

WHY A BOOK ON THE FLORA OF GROOTBOS?

Back in 1991, the Lutzeyer family purchased a 123 hectare farm on the slopes overlooking Walker Bay between the villages of Stanford and Gansbaai. At the time Michael and his wife Dorothee were won over by the spectacular sea views and visions of family weekends spent on the farm with horses, pigs and fresh veggies, while the pink fields of flowering wild malva went a long way to convincing Michael's parents, Heiner and Eva, that this was a worthwhile investment for their retirement. Little did they realise at the time that they were making their first step in establishing what would become Grootbos Nature Reserve – a 2 500 hectare botanical treasure trove, wildlife sanctuary and a world leader in luxury responsible tourism.

From left to right: *Tertius, Gabi, Dorothee and Michael Lutzeyer*

Michael with his children Sanja and Jan at Grootbos in the early days.

The beautiful Lachenalia lutzeyeri, *a rare endemic plant species found only on Grootbos Nature Reserve.*

Over the years we have gradually deciphered the complexities of the flora, exploring every nook and cranny of the reserve and unearthing some quite remarkable botanical finds. We now know that Grootbos is a haven of protection for many rare and threatened plants. The unique combination of its many habitat 'niches', regular fires, nutrient poor soils and the huge variety of insect pollinators has resulted in an explosion of speciation in the Cape, a botanical wonderland unmatched on Earth. Yet all around us human greed continues to plunder these landscapes and within just a few generations may destroy what has taken millions of years to form.

Grootbos and its partners in the Walker Bay Fynbos Conservancy are determined to protect, restore and promote the crucial natural corridor linking the Walker Bay coastline to other important conservation areas inland on the Agulhas Plain. For us every tiny piece of natural veld is valuable and, as we have shown on Grootbos, any remnant piece of natural vegetation in the Cape is highly likely to contain special plants and even some as yet unidentified species.

It is our hope that as you page through this book showcasing some of the plants found on one relatively small area overlooking Walker Bay, you too will marvel at the floral diversity of the Cape and be inspired to care for and protect the diversity of life on our planet.

GROOTBOS NATURE RESERVE

Historical background

Human occupation of this region dates back to prehistoric times, with one of South Africa's most important coastal middle stone-age cave dwelling sites, the Klipgat Cave, situated less than 5 km from Grootbos on the Walker Bay coastline.

The Klipgat Cave on the Walker Bay coastline has been home to humans for more than 60 000 years.

Early Stone Age implements found on Grootbos have been estimated to be over 250 000 years of age. The Grootbos landscape has been traversed and inhabited by humans throughout mankind's history, and the associated hunting, agricultural and other human impacts have varied with each passing society. Early human societies would have lived a subsistence existence of hunter-gatherers. These people and more recent pastoralists, the Khoi khoi people, possibly made considerable use of fire as a management tool to increase the grazing potential of the veld for wildlife and domestic livestock. However, the most recent European society has had the greatest ecological impact on the landscape. The introduction of mechanised agricultural practices, the large scale removal of timber from Milkwood and other forests for building and industry, the development of urban landscapes and infrastructure, and the intentional planting of invasive Australian and European plants have only occurred in this region during the past 100 years with huge negative impact on biodiversity.

Grootbos farm was granted to its first owner, Dirk Cloete, on 18 April 1831, who paid the princely sum of one pound and sixteen shillings sterling for the property. The Sir Lowry's Pass over the Hottentots-Holland Mountains had been inaugurated the previous year, opening up easier access to the region. The farm was then known as Baviaans Fontein and was 2 198 hectares in extent. The original farmhouse on Baviaans Fontein (our neighbour en route to Flower Valley) was built in approximately 1840. Over the years that followed the property was divided up into smaller portions. One of these was the 123 hectare property, including the Grootbos Milkwood forest, which was purchased by the Lutzeyer family in 1991. The Lutzeyers originally used Grootbos as a family holiday farm visiting the house (which is now the Garden Lodge kitchen, and staff canteen) virtually every weekend and holiday.

In 1994 Michael decided to sell his business interests in Cape Town and develop a bed & breakfast guest farm for local patrons. Joined by his brother and sister-in-law, Tertius and Gabi Lutzeyer, the guest farm grew rapidly into an international five-star eco-lodge. From the beginning the Lutzeyers realised the importance of basing the business on the region's spectacular natural beauty and diverse flora and fauna. The lodge and guest suites were carefully integrated into the natural environment, local artisans and craftsman were employed, and the farm registered as a private nature reserve. Already at this early stage the foundations were being established to grow the business into a world leader in responsible nature-based tourism.

Using local artisans and craftsmen, Garden Lodge was built to blend into the natural environment.

Between 1991 and 2010 Grootbos has grown from the first 123 hectare farm to now include seven farms totalling 2 500 hectares of conservation land. Much of this land had previously been poorly managed as cattle and flower harvesting farms to the detriment of the region's biodiversity, and provided few livelihood opportunities. Over the years Grootbos staff have cleared all alien vegetation from the property, restored damaged areas and now manage the land according to strict ecological principles. The tourism development and associated non-profit programmes of the Grootbos Foundation now employ in excess of 150 full time staff, some 80% of whom are from local disadvantaged communities.

The Lodges

Garden Lodge was built during 1996 and designed to blend into the natural surroundings by using stone and thatch and maximising the sweeping views across Walker Bay. The original farm house that now forms the kitchen and service area of the lodge was originally surrounded by large kikuyu grazing lawns. The grass was removed, ponds and walkways constructed and thousands of indigenous plants propagated and used to rehabilitate this area into a beautiful indigenous garden. The 11 luxury, free-standing suites were carefully placed in natural gaps on the edge of the ancient Grootbos Milkwood forest. Each of these units is stylishly furnished with

luxurious canopy beds, spacious en-suite bathrooms, separate lounges with cosy fireplaces and wooden decks with spectacular views across the bay.

Guest occupancies grew rapidly to a point where it was decided to build a second lodge on the reserve. A site with equally spectacular views and another ancient Milkwood forest was chosen on the hills to the south of Garden Lodge. The magnificent Forest Lodge opened its doors to its first guests in the spring of 2004. It had a sophisticated contemporary design and consisted of a main lodge with restaurant, bars, spacious lounge area, gallery, infinity pool and conference centre as well as

Garden Lodge was carefully constructed on the edge of the Grootbos milkwood forest.

10 luxurious, freestanding suites tucked away on the fringe of the forest. The lodge and luxury suites have fantastic views across the fynbos, dunes and ocean. The free-standing suites were carefully located beneath the overhang of Milkwood trees, providing the ideal blend of privacy and comfort.

Unfortunately less than a year and half after opening to its first guests, the entire Grootbos Reserve was engulfed in a huge wild fire that started on a farm near Elim, some 50 kilometres to the east. The fire raged for more than a week, reaching the Grootbos lodges simultaneously on 1 February 2006. While Garden Lodge was spared with minor damage, Forest Lodge as well as three of its suites was totally destroyed.

Above: *The original Forest Lodge was completed in the spring of 2004 and had a thatch roof.*
Below: *The remains of Forest Lodge on 2 February 2006.*

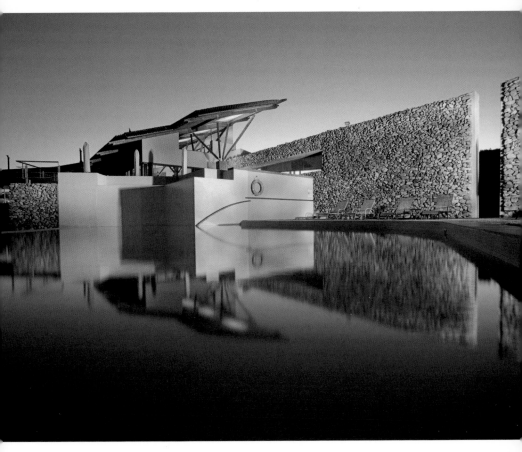

The magnificent new Forest Lodge was rebuilt by October 2006 and features a slate roof.

The day after the fire, work began on rebuilding Grootbos. Garden Lodge, which had suffered minor damages, was re-opened to guests after two weeks. Quite unbelievably, under the guidance of Tertius Lutzeyer, Forest Lodge, the three burnt suites and six new suites at Forest Lodge were simultaneously re-opened to guests at the beginning of October that year.

The latest addition to the Grootbos portfolio is the Villa. Surrounded by fynbos, the Villa consists of six elegant suites with 180° views over Walker Bay. Here guests can relax in over one thousand square metres of utter luxury and privacy, which includes two lounge areas, a private dining room, a media room, wine cellar, outside BBQ area, private pool as well as a fully-equipped kitchen. Guests at the Villa have the luxury of their own private guide, chef and butler and complete privacy to enjoy all that Grootbos has to offer.

The Grootbos Villa provides over 1 000m² of exquisite, private luxury in a spectacular setting.

GROOTBOS GUIDED ACTIVITIES

Visits to Grootbos provide a wonderful opportunity to experience and learn about all the area has to offer. Guests are accompanied on all activities by specialist guides, some of whom have worked their way up through the ranks from the Green Futures training programme on Grootbos. The guiding philosophy at Grootbos aims to convert science into stories in such a way that nature comes to life for the guests. At the same time the threats posed to the region's delicate biodiversity are emphasised, as is the role that Grootbos and its conservation partners are playing in countering these threats. Tours take place on Grootbos and to sites of interest in the general vicinity of the reserve.

Grootbos Nature Reserve tours

Guided nature tours of Grootbos take guests through a mosaic of different habitats including a variety of different fynbos and forest vegetation types. Milkwood forest walks lead guests into the heart of these ancient forests where they learn about the forest history, ecology and fascinating ecosystems. Fynbos tours focus on the amazing diversity of the region's flora, its unique and threatened species, interactions between the plants and animals, the role of fire in fynbos ecology and the interesting combination of factors responsible for its fragile existence. These tours can be undertaken on foot, by 4x4 vehicles or on horseback.

Horse riding

The 2 500 hectare Grootbos Reserve and neighbouring Walker Bay coastline provide excellent opportunities for horse riding. Grootbos has its own stables with 16 well-trained horses as well as foals and ponies for children's rides. Experienced horse riding instructors lead these tours through the reserve and cater for all levels of riding experience, including complete novices. Horse riding on Grootbos is a wonderful way of experiencing the beauty of the fynbos, surrounded by the flowers and birds unique to our region. Panoramic views of the surrounding mountains and seascapes make for a great nature experience. Grootbos guests can also join longer beach horse riding excursions to Walker Bay Nature Reserve. The route takes riders through the dune fynbos to the beach where they can enjoy gallops or gentle cantering next to the waves.

Coastal tours, Klipgat Cave and whale watching

The Walker Bay coastline offers spectacular scenery, wide open beaches, cultural and historically important caves and wonderful opportunities to watch and learn about the whales and other marine life found in the area. Between June and December Walker Bay is home to high concentrations of Southern right whales. These magnificent creatures migrate between the Antarctic and the southern coastlines of South America, South Africa and Australia. They spend approximately half of the year (roughly December until May/June) in the Antarctic region where feeding is their main objective. Having stocked up on food reserves, they migrate north between 3 000–4 000 km to their mating and breeding grounds. One of their favoured localities is Walker Bay where they approach to within metres of the rocky shoreline.

The Klipgat Cave provides a window into pre-historic times and provides insight into changing climates and sea levels. For at least 60 000 years our human ancestors have lived along the Walker Bay coastline. The Klipgat Cave provided the perfect summer time shelter, protecting its inhabitants from harsh coastal winds and was closely located to an abundant supply of fresh seafood and spring water. The remains of this habitation are amongst the earliest in the world belonging to modern people (*Homo sapiens sapiens*). These people lived off the land and sea, on eland, black wildebeest and other mammals and collected plants, tortoises, shellfish, seals and birds. About 2 000 years ago, early herders may also have inhabited the cave. They left stone and bone artefacts and ornaments, as well as some of the earliest sheep bones in the Western Cape and some of the oldest pottery in South Africa.

Southern right whales can be seen within metres of the cliffs along the Walker Bay shoreline every year from June to December.

The magnificent Walker Bay has long been home to our human ancestors, and has been preserved as one of the most pristine natural areas along the Cape coastline.

Archaeologists have uncovered some remarkable information regarding the way of life of these early inhabitants as well as information on changing climates and sea level changes through excavations in the Klipgat Cave.

Boat trips to Dyer Island and boat-based whale watching

Dyer Island is a 20 hectare nature reserve, situated 8.5 km from Kleinbaai harbour in Gansbaai. The island is recognised as an Important Bird Area (IBA), and is home to thousands of Cape fur seals as well as endangered African penguins, Bank cormorant and Roseate tern. Other breeding species include the Cape, White-breasted and Crowned cormorants, Leach's storm petrel, African black oystercatchers and Kelp and Hartlaub's gulls. Grootbos uses the services of the Dyer Island Cruises company to take its guests to the island on a marine eco-safari. Dyer Island Cruises is focused on the conservation of the marine environment around Dyer Island (see www.dict.org.za) and offers a complete nature experience including the island's unique bird life, the African penguins, Cape fur seals and surface viewing of the Great white shark.

During whale season, the Dyer Island Cruises boat trip offers guests the opportunity to view Southern right whales from the boat. Only 22 licences have been issued for boat-based whale watching along the South African coastline. Four of these licences were issued for the Walker Bay area. The boats are permitted to come within 50 metres of the whales. As these gentle giants are very curious, they often swim right up to the boat to get a better view of the boat and the guests!

Boat-based whale watching provides an unforgettable nature experience.

Shark cage diving

Gansbaai has the reputation of being the white shark capital of the world. Divers and adventurer travellers from all over the world come to watch Great white sharks in the waters around Dyer Island. Every day a number of boats leave Kleinbaai harbour to spend a few hours on the water to view the Great white sharks from the boat or to go cage diving to view these amazing creatures in their underwater habitat.

Watsonia schlechteri *and* Bobartia indica *blooming in mountain fynbos following fire on Grootbos.*

THE FYNBOS

The Cape Floristic Region is home to one of the richest floras in the world. Within an area of just under 91 000 km² there are 9 250 species of flowering plants, some 70% of which are restricted to the region. Fynbos is the major element of this region, contributing more than 80% of its species. The region also includes renosterveld, karroid shrubland, thicket and forests. Fynbos is not only famous for its remarkable diversity, but also the beauty of many of its wildflowers. It is found at the southern tip of Africa in roughly a crescent shaped belt from Vanrhynsdorp in the north, southwards to the Cape Peninsula and eastwards to Port Elizabeth. Fynbos is largely restricted to the distribution of the parallel sandstone and quartzitic formations of the Cape Fold Mountains and the extensive areas of sand and limestone along the coast. Here it thrives on coarse-grained soils that are low in nutrients, especially nitrogen and phosphorous. It is predominantly found in the winter rainfall region of the Cape, although there are areas in the Eastern Cape, where fynbos thrives, that are characterised by year-round rainfall. The main reason for the exceptional diversity in fynbos is not an unusually high concentration of species in a particular site, but rather the high proportion of turnover in species between sites. This is the result of the high rate at which species give way to each other across environmental and geographical gradients. So what makes fynbos really special is its exceptionally high numbers of localised species, often restricted to a single, small area, sometimes less than 1 km². Grootbos alone is home to at least four endemic species.

Fynbos and fire

Fynbos is a fire-adapted vegetation that requires regular burning for its persistence. In the absence of fire, fynbos is gradually replaced by thicket species. It thrives on infertile soils and fire is the mechanism that recycles precious nutrients from old moribund growth into the soil. Fire in fynbos is far from a disaster, but rather a crucial trigger that resets the fynbos 'successional clock'. It provides the stimulus for dormant seeds to germinate and the opportunity for many annuals, short-lived perennials and bulbs to grow, flower and seed during times of abundant nutrients and sunlight. These plants complete their short life cycles, return to the soil as the larger shrubs overwhelm them, and remain dormant until the next fire. The optimal fire cycle for fynbos is between 10-14 years. Shorter fire cycles can wipe out slow maturing species, while species start dying when intervals become too long.

Fynbos conservation

The unique flora of the Cape is under severe pressure from human activities. The fynbos of the mountainous areas is generally well protected in a considerable reserve network established to ensure plentiful supplies of clean drinking water for the region's growing human population. Unfortunately, the same cannot be said for the lowlands. Here, centuries of intensive agriculture have resulted in monocultures over almost all of the more fertile areas. On the Agulhas Plain, some 25% of lowland fynbos has been transformed by agriculture, and of the remaining habitat, the majority is invaded to some degree by Australian wattles and other invasive species. The wattles were planted in order to stabilise coastal dune fields during the mid-twentieth century and have subsequently spread into the fynbos, outcompeting and throttling the indigenous flora. Critically almost all of the lowlands are in private ownership and only about 5% is formally conserved. Other threats include rapidly escalating urbanisation, especially coastal resort development, drainage of wetlands, inappropriate fire regimes and unsustainable flower harvesting. Socio economic issues are amplifying the effect of these threats. For generations the plight of poor rural communities has been largely ignored. In many of the towns and villages poverty is rife and as much as half of the inhabitants are unemployed.

Effective conservation of the remaining natural areas will only be possible if fynbos can earn its keep. And this will only happen if we can find ways to deliver better financial returns from natural fynbos landscapes than other land use practices, if natural resources can be made more accessible to the poor and all people can be educated to its uniqueness and value. At Grootbos our conservation efforts are therefore focused on tackling these issues of economic incentives and social upliftment through the work of the Grootbos Foundation.

THE GROOTBOS FOUNDATION

From the beginning, the owners of Grootbos have been committed to the conservation of the region's biodiversity as well as the upliftment of local communities. The non-profit Grootbos Foundation was established during 2004 to run the Grootbos environmental and social development programme and has as its mission:

The conservation of biodiversity of Grootbos and its surrounds
and development of sustainable nature based livelihoods through ecotourism,
research, management and education.

Funds generated by the Grootbos ecotourism business, together with donations received from guests and other donors are invested through the foundation into implementing key conservation and development projects. In this way all Grootbos guests are directly supporting biodiversity conservation and social upliftment in the Walker Bay region.

The foundation also aims to run most of its projects as self-sustaining entities that generate their own income through the sale of home grown products.

Green Futures

The Green Futures Horticulture and Life Skills College provides an annual training programme on Grootbos to 12 unemployed youths from the Gansbaai area in horticulture, indigenous gardening and life skills development. The course has been running since 2003 and all graduates have found employment on completion of the course. This is testament to the success of this unique training model developed by Grootbos personnel. The horticultural component of the course includes plant identification, an appreciation of fynbos and its ecology, why and how it can be preserved, how to use it in indigenous gardening, fynbos propagation and nursery skills, garden design, as well as garden establishment and maintenance using water-wise techniques. All theory is backed up by a range of practical work in developing and maintaining gardens on Grootbos and for private clients. The sale of plants and provision of landscaping services by the students provides income to the college. In

The Green Futures college and nursery on Grootbos. A wide range of indigenous plants that have been grown by the students are sold from the nursery to raise funds for the project.

this way, through their labour, students help to pay for their own tuition. The life skills component of the course includes a first aid course, numeracy skills, literacy skills, health issues, an AIDS awareness programme, interpersonal skills, money management, basic computer skills, basic business skills as well as completing a driver's license. The life skills component of the course has proven vital in assisting graduates to successfully find employment. In addition to the education curriculum, the college provides transport, breakfast and lunch, uniforms, equipment and a basic wage to students. Every year, three of the best students are given the opportunity to visit and work at the Eden Project (www.edenproject.com) in Cornwall, U.K. This is an amazing opportunity that opens their eyes to our dependence on plants and the natural world. The rest of the students are also provided with fascinating experiential training opportunities at Kirstenbosch and Harold Porter National Botanical Gardens. On completion of their course, the students are awarded a nationally accredited certificate in horticulture and are assisted in work placement.

Gansbaai sport and youth development programme

Michael Lutzeyer first realised the need for quality sports facilities in Gansbaai whilst watching his son playing soccer for the Green Futures team. Some 17 clubs played on a sandy, dusty depression in the Gansbaai township of Masakhane. The field was in a shocking state and there was little, if any, opportunity for younger children to play the game they adore. Instead they were confined to playing in adjacent township streets. Following an intensive networking and fundraising campaign by Michael, the Gansbaai sports facility was launched in April 2008 with the assistance of the Overstrand Municipality, Absa Bank and the Western Cape Department of Cultural

Affairs and Sport; complete with a 3G, full size artificial soccer pitch sponsored by the English Premier League. The project was developed on municipal land situated between the traditional black, white and coloured areas of Gansbaai.

Michael's dream did not end with the construction of quality sporting facilities. Instead the focus of the Grootbos Foundation shifted to ensuring that these facilities were optimally utilised for the development and integration of our youth. With the support of the English Premier League, the Football Foundation of South Africa (FFSA) was established in partnership with the Grootbos Foundation to run youth development programmes at the sports centre. Under the excellent guidance of project manager Lean Terblanche, Michael's dream of bringing different communities together through sport had been realised. The project provides young people from all communities with quality sporting facilities, equipment and coaches. The programme comprises training five days per week, with games, tournaments and coaching clinics taking place on weekends. Dedicated coaches and volunteers run football, netball, hockey and cricket coaching sessions for the region's youngsters, developing boys and girls from the age six through to 19. Holiday programmes are a highlight on the programme's calendar, and attract children from the entire community for weeks of fun, games and educational activities. Awareness programmes are launched around important days in South Africa such as Youth Day, Women's Day, Freedom Day and World Aids Day. The children learn about significant events in history, as well as pertinent social and environmental issues.

The program brings children from different communities together and provides quality sporting facilities, equipment and coaches.

Through sports these boys and girls are learning life skills, discipline and respect; they are exercising, building their self-esteem and self-confidence, and interacting with other communities. Most of all, these children are doing what they love most in a safe environment with positive role models. Sport is a wonderful way of breaking down barriers and this project has helped to unite youngsters in the region – regardless of their social and economic background, race or gender.

Growing the Future

Following the success of the Green Futures model, the Grootbos Foundation launched the Growing the Future Food Production and Life Skills College on Women's Day in 2009. This training programme aims to uplift women from the Stanford community, training eight woman each year in vegetable growing, fruit, beekeeping and the principles of successful animal husbandry. Subsistence farming has always been integral to many South African cultures, but in recent years, as people have moved from rural areas to the cities in search of work, many of these skills have been lost. The training programme is 30% theoretical and 70% practical. The vegetable growing training focuses on organic farming techniques and the women are trained in basic soil science, soil improvement and preparation, propagation techniques, planting and care of vegetables, seasonal planting, inter-planting, basic permaculture concepts, organic feeding and pest control regimes. The women also receive practical training in the farming of free-range eggs, free-range pig farming, beekeeping as well as

The Growing the Future project provides training to women from disadvantaged backgrounds in food production and life skills.

in jam and preserve making. About half of the course content focuses on life skills including literacy and numeracy, health and safety issues, an HIV/AIDS awareness programme, basic computer skills, book keeping, money management and business planning. The students are fully equipped, have access to transport and receive a weekly stipend for living expenses from the foundation.

The produce from the project is sold by the foundation to the Grootbos lodge kitchens, surrounding restaurants and at a local organic market. In this way the women's labour pays towards their tuition, Grootbos knows where and how its fresh produce has been grown and Grootbos guests can see how their food is being locally and organically produced.

The Future Trees Project

The 2006 fire on Grootbos not only destroyed Forest Lodge, but also a large area of the ancient Milkwood forest behind the lodge. The fire struck the forest at midday, having burnt for more than a week under extremely hot and dry conditions. The result was that a large portion of the forest, including many ancient trees, was destroyed by the fire. The Future Trees Project aims to rehabilitate this area as well as other forest areas on Grootbos that have been impacted by human activities in the past. Early aerial photographs have provided a clear indication of changes to the forest edges as a result of human impacts, primarily wood cutting and exotic tree invasions over the last 80 years. Appropriate indigenous trees have been grown by the Green Futures students to be used for the rehabilitation of these areas. Visitors to Grootbos can support the rehabilitation of these ancient Milkwood forests as well as contribute to the work of the foundation by getting their hands dirty and planting a tree. Already nearly 1 000 indigenous trees have been planted as part of this programme, their location recorded by GPS and uploaded via the Grootbos Foundation website onto Google Earth.

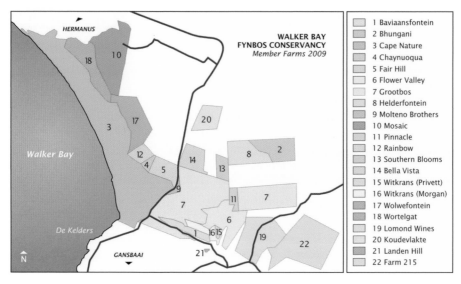

The members of the Walker Bay fynbos conservancy in 2009.

The Walker Bay Fynbos Conservancy

From an early stage in the development of Grootbos, it became clear that effective conservation of the region's biodiversity would require looking beyond our borders and developing partnerships with our neighbours. As a result, in 1999 Grootbos became one of the first members of the Walker Bay Fynbos Conservancy (www.fynbos. co.za). This role model public/private conservation partnership has brought together 22 landowners collectively owning 12 179 hectares of coastal and mountain fynbos, which is being jointly managed for conservation. In partnership with other conservancy members, conservation, fire reaction, alien clearing and tourism management plans for the conservancy have been developed. These will ensure continuity in the management of the area, the creation of new tourism attractions and increased access to natural resources and employment opportunities for local communities. The Grootbos Foundation is working closely with its partners in the conservancy to document the region's flora and fauna. Some 850 species of indigenous plants have been recorded in the conservancy and it is estimated that this will rise to close to 1 000 species once a full botanical survey of the area has been undertaken. There is also a high diversity of fauna within the conservancy. Two hundred and forty nine birds, 66 mammals, 53 reptiles, 21 amphibians and numerous invertebrate species have been recorded. It is clear that the future security of the unique biodiversity of the Walker Bay region will be dependent on further strengthening of these partnerships and a growing commitment to collaborative conservation planning and implementation.

THE GEOLOGY, TOPOGRAPHY AND SOILS OF GROOTBOS

The deposition of coarse-grained sand particles which would become the underlying sandstone base of the reserve began about 500 million years ago along a passive continental margin. Deep burial cemented the sand into sandstone. This Table Mountain Sandstone has been very important in shaping the region's ecology, as soils derived from these sandstones are poor in nutrients, especially phosphorous and nitrogen. Had these underlying soils been richer in nutrients, as is the case inland towards Caledon, they would almost certainly have been ploughed up for agriculture. The Cape mountains, including our underlying topography and peaks such as Swartkransberg and Witkransberg, were formed about 250 million years ago when the South American and Antarctic continents collided with that of Africa, to form the then single continent of Pangaea. This uprising event ended some 200 million years ago. What we see today is only the worn-down remnants of what was once a much larger mountain chain.

The last few million years have been characterised by a succession of ice ages. Many parts of the world, including northern Europe, were under ice sheets that completely obliterated the flora. In the Cape, permanent ice sheets only covered the highest peaks and the flora of Grootbos would not have been seriously impacted. This is one of the reasons for the high diversity of the Cape flora. During these glaciation events, millions of litres of water would have been tied up in the enlarged polar ice caps. As a result the sea level would have dropped by up to 125 metres. Walker Bay was exposed leaving a large dry plain with a very different coastline some 100 kilometres further out to sea. During the warmer interglacial periods the polar ice caps partially melted, causing the sea level to rise about 25 metres above its present levels.

As reflected in the vegetation communities found at Grootbos and shown on the map on the inside cover of this book, other more recent formations overlay the Table Mountain Sandstone. These significantly influence the composition of the flora on the reserve. Most extensive is a deep covering of calcareous wind-blown sand with a pH range of 6.5 to 8 on the lower slopes (up to 277 m amsl.). This has been deposited within the last several million to several thousand years. Another overlay is the Bredasdorp Limestone Formation, a conglomeration of calcified marine/freshwater organism remains deposited during times of higher-than-present sea levels between

25 and 10 million years ago. Also dating back to this period are areas of ferricrete formed through clay-soil weathering. The Table Mountain Sandstone is exposed on the higher slopes and hilltops with associated acidic soils (pH 5.5). The two highest mountain peaks on the reserve are Protea Peak (Swartkransberg 514 m amsl) and God's Window (Witkransberg 451 m amsl). The peak of Swartkransberg is the property of the Flower Valley Conservation Trust. The small seepage zones and wetlands support more organically rich soils and the only perennial river is located on Witvoetskloof.

THE GROOTBOS VEGETATION SURVEY

When travelling along the main road between Stanford and Gansbaai and looking up at the green hills to the east one could be forgiven for thinking that the vegetation is rather dull and boring. I first arrived at Grootbos in January 1997, fresh from completing a study of the fynbos growing on very similar habitats at Cape Point Nature Reserve, some 90 km to the west. The differences in the flora between Grootbos and Cape Point were immediately apparent, despite their obvious similarities in geology, soils and climate. As I took my first guided tours of the reserve with inquisitive guests, I was amazed at the diverse habitats and associated species wealth. It quickly became apparent that a full vegetation survey including a species checklist and vegetation-environment analysis was needed for the reserve. In the winter of 1997 we carefully selected sites for 50, 5 x 10m permanent vegetation plots, chosen to include all the obvious habitats on Grootbos. We carefully recorded species and abundances as well as environmental characteristics for each plot. We also recorded all species on our journeys between the plots and while driving around the reserve. The result was a first vegetation map for Grootbos and a list of 250 plant species, of which 31 had Red Data Book status, meaning they were species of conservation concern. One of the species, *Erica magnisylvae*, found tucked away on a few south facing slopes of the reserve, was new to science.

The author in a thick stand of Erica magnisylvae *shortly after its discovery on Grootbos in 1997.*

This study was used to extrapolate what the total number of flowering species on the reserve was likely to be and came up with a figure of between 330 and 377 species. At around this time, three major conservation planning exercises were being completed for the Agulhas Plain, and in all three Grootbos was deemed to be an area of low conservation value. According to the available data at the time Grootbos and the surrounding Walker Bay region appeared to lack endemic species and unique habitats, had an impoverished and unremarkable Proteaceae flora – in one of the studies the Protea family was used as a key indicator of botanical wealth – and did not boast unique or rare ecological and evolutionary processes.

However, we did not stop there and have continued collecting, identifying and photographing the flora of Grootbos ever since. Initially species were added to our list as they were recorded on guided tours and occasional walks through the reserve. The picture changed considerably as Heiner Lutzeyer became more interested in studying the flora. Initially, it was his interest in photography and the desire to know what he was photographing that increased the reserve's plant list. Subsequently he has become an ardent amateur botanist and specialist of all that is green on Grootbos. The result is a unique vegetation study, quite possibly the most detailed ever undertaken in the fynbos region, which has continued from 1997 to the present, included all seasons and all stages of post-fire succession on the reserve. The results have been staggering. Between 1997 and early 2010 the number of positively identified, herbarium-catalogued plant species on Grootbos has increased to 765 – at least twice the number estimated from the earlier plot data. Sixty-seven of the additional species that have been found are species of conservation concern, while a further five species new to science have been recorded. The deeply significant ecological role of fire in fynbos was emphasised by the way the checklist jumped from 680 to 750 species after the huge 2006 blaze that swept through Grootbos – 70 new species for our list as a result of post-fire successional processes.

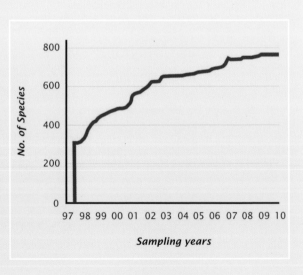

The species accumulation curve showing the increase in the total number of indigenous plant species recorded on Grootbos between 1997 and 2010. The steep accumulation at the beginning was the result of the original vegetation survey undertaken on the reserve. (adapted from Cowling et al. 2010)

NEW PLANT SPECIES FIRST RECORDED ON GROOTBOS

A total of six species new to science have been recorded during our vegetation survey of the reserve. These are briefly described below and fully described in the main identification section of the guide.

Erica magnisylvae
(Ericaceae: *see page 202 for full description*)

This species was first found by Sean Privett on Grootbos during the original vegetation survey of the reserve in the winter of 1997. It was described by Ted Oliver of the Compton Herbarium who named it with reference to its discovery on Grootbos; *magnisylvae* = of the large forest in classical Latin. It has so far only been recorded on Grootbos with an outlying population on the damp slopes above Platbos Forest to the south east.

Cliffortia anthospermoides
(Rosaceae: *see page 148 for full description*)

At first sight this species may be mistaken for a member of the genus Anthospermum (Rubiaceae), hence its species name anthospermoides. It was first discovered by Anna Fellingham on Grootbos Nature Reserve in Overberg dune strandveld vegetation in 1996. Only four populations are known, all on or in close vicinity to Grootbos and only the population on Grootbos is protected.

Lachenalia lutzeyeri
(Hyacinthaceae: *see page 106 for full description*)

This species was first collected by Heiner Lutzeyer on the upper slopes of Witkransberg after a small fire in November 2004. It only flowers in the early summer following fire and is presently only known from the type locality on Witkransberg on Grootbos.

Pterygodium vermiferum
(Orchidaceae: *see page 64 for full description*)

First recorded on Grootbos on the path up to Swartkransberg at an altitude of 385 m by Heiner Lutzeyer in 2003. Subsequent collections have been made on these western slopes of the mountain at three separate sites about 260 m apart. A second population is located along the road between Stanford and Gansbaai and a third population is at Die Kelders at an altitude of 50 m. The total known area of extent of this species measures just 5.5 by 3.0 km along an L-shaped range, the majority of which is conserved within the Grootbos Reserve!

Capnophyllum lutzeyeri
(Apiaceae: *see page 266 for full description*)

This species has only ever been recorded on Grootbos. It was first located following the 2006 fire on acidic soils. No plants were found in subsequent searches suggesting that it is a short-lived, fire-induced, species.

Dasispermum grandicarpum
(Apiaceae: *see page 268 for full description*)

It is known only from Grootbos, where it was first collected by Heiner Lutzeyer in 2007 in fynbos vegetation that had burnt the previous year. No plants could be located in subsequent searches suggesting that the species may be a short-lived species, germinating, flowering and dying in the first year following fire.

In addition to these new species recorded on Grootbos, our vegetation survey has resulted in many significant range extensions for species previously not known from the area. This new information has added extensively to our knowledge of the flora of the Agulhas Plain. Other exciting botanical discoveries have been made in the Walker Bay Conservancy area including the discovery of *Aloe juddii* (left), a new Aloe species on the upper, rocky sandstone slopes of Farm 215 and Flower Valley.

It is important to stress that there is nothing in the biophysical conditions at Grootbos and surrounding area that would make botanists anticipate such 'astonishing results', and that similar detailed, long-term studies elsewhere in the Cape flora are likely to produce similar results. It is quite clear that given enough time for botanising we will find that every bit of remaining natural veld is important for conservation!

PLANT COMMUNITIES ON GROOTBOS

Milkwood forest

The Milkwood forests belong to the most conspicious elements of Grootbos, constituting a sharp contrast to the fynbos covering the vast majority of the reserve. These Western Cape Milkwood forests have recently been categorised as an endangered vegetation type as result of their small geographic extent and high level of threats. Four large patches are present at Tygerboom and Grootbos in the south, Steynsbos in the north and Witvoetskloof in the north east. One smaller pocket is located adjacent to the Steynsbos dam. Altogether some 60 ha of Grootbos is covered by Milkwood forest. It is an indicator of the value of these forests that their names were chosen to name some of the farms making up the reserve today. As a result of their distinctive character and position overlooking Walker Bay both Garden and Forest Lodges were built on the periphery of these forests. White Milkwood (*Sideroxylon inerme*), is widespread in coastal forests and thickets along the southern and eastern coastline of South Africa, but this type of forest is restricted to the Stanford-Gansbaai-area, with the only protected patches being on Grootbos. They are characterised by deep, sandy, colluvial soils with high levels of calcium and phosphorous.

The pH ranges from 6.3 to 7.9, with a peak around 7.5. The high levels of mineral components appear to be a distinctive feature of this type of ecosystem. Calcium in particular is considerably richer in the Milkwood forests than anywhere else on the reserve. In addition, the soils are more fertile due to plant-induced organic enrichment. This has resulted in clearing for agriculture in the past, most notably

The 23 hectare Grootbos Milkwood forest with Garden Lodge suites to the left.

the eastern extent of Grootbos Forest and a large piece of Platbos Forest directly to the east. The forests are characterised by a single tree layer to about 6 m, usually dominated by *Sideroxylon inerme*. The gnarled trunks of old individuals give the forest its unique ambience. The oldest individuals are estimated to be over 800 years of age. Other tree species in the forest are *Euclea racemosa*, *Chionanthus foveolatus*, *Gymnosporia buxifolia* and the winter-deciduous *Celtis africana*, but none of these achieve dominance.

The soil is covered by a 5–30 cm high herb layer, which is very sparse in deeply shaded places but can constitute a dense ground cover where more light penetrates the tree canopy. *Droguetia iners* dominates in most places and is accompanied by the grass *Ehrharta erecta*. The only true shrub species within the full shade of the forest is *Myrsine africana*, which can grow taller than 1 m. In damp sites the arum lily *Zantedeschia aethiopica* can also reach a considerable height. The climbers *Asparagus aethiopicus*, *Cynanchum obtusifolium*, *Kedrostis nana* and *Zehneria scabra* are common in the forest. Compared to the surrounding fynbos, the species diversity is low with a total of only 44 plant species having been recorded in these forests. They are considered to be a late successional stage of dune strandveld.

Afromontane Forest

The Afromontane forests on Grootbos are located in steep, south-facing ravines that are largely protected from fire. Six patches of afromontane forest of different sizes can be found on Grootbos altogether covering approximately seven hectares of the reserve. They occur at sites with shallow, neutral to slightly acidic soils that contain high levels of potassium and magnesium. The forests form tall canopies up to 15 m high frequently dominated by *Rapanea melanophloeos*. Other dominant species are *Olinia ventosa*, *Adopytes dimidiata* and *Kiggelaria africana*. The sub-canopy is three to six metres high and includes *Chionanthus foveolatus*, *Sideroxylon inerme* and *Diospyros whyteana*. These species can also grow to full canopy height in places. The ground layer is usually sparse with *Asplenium adiantum-nigrum*, *Droguetia iners* and *Ehrharta erecta* the most common species. The climbers *Asparagus aethiopicus*, *A. scandens*, *Rhoicissus tomentosa* and *Cynanchum obtusifolium* are fairly abundant. The Afromontane forests of the Agulhas Plain are ecologically similar but floristically distinct from those of the mountains further north. They show affinities to the dune forests of the Tongaland- Pondoland Forests. These forests, and the afromontane forests along the south coast (Knysna, Tsitsikamma), have significantly higher species diversity than the forests on Grootbos. One forest with a higher species composition is that growing along the perennial stream at Witvoetskloof. This forest patch has species such as *Ocotea bullata*, *Cunonia capensis* and *Curtisia dentata* that are not found on the drier forest patches elsewhere in the reserve.

A striking feature of the Afromontane and Milkwood forests of Grootbos is their low alpha (or site)-diversity, especially when compared with the adjacent fynbos.

From a floristic point of view, the forest is a completely different system, having virtually no species at all in common with fynbos and hosting no species endemic to the Cape Floristic Region. The absence of elements typical of the Cape flora underlines the distinct nature of these forest environments. This phenomenon is closely related to the fact that unlike fynbos, afromontane forests are fire-free ecosystems, the species are not flammable but their regeneration is connected to extended fire-free periods.

Overberg dune strandveld

The entire western side of Grootbos and much of Walker Bay is covered in an extensive matrix of Overberg dune strandveld vegetation. This vegetation type occurs on deep, marine-derived calcareous soils of relatively recent origin. The pH of the sandy soils range between 7.9 and 8.1 and they are mostly more than 100 m deep. This vegetation type occurs on flat or slightly undulating dune lowlands from Rooiels in the Cape Hangklip area to as far east as Cape Infanta at the mouth of the Breede River.

The afromontane forests have tall canopies up to 15 m high.

The vegetation is dominated by *Metalasia muricata*, *Metalasia densa*, *Passerina corymbosa*, *Anthospermum aethiopicum*, *Osteospermum moniliferum* and *Aspalathus forbesii*. The local endemic *Erica irregularis* is also common, turning the hill slopes pink in autumn and winter. Among the restioids, the large tufted *Thamnochortus erectus* is most conspicuous and the lower *Ischyrolepis eleocharis* is a very common groundcover. A characteristic feature of the strandveld is the lack of proteoids. In the absence of fire this vegetation type is transitional to thicket. *Euclea racemosa*, *Olea capensis ssp. capensis*, *Olea exasperata* and *Rhus laevigata* are common. Where fire has been exluded for an extended period, such as along roads or adjacent to cultivated areas or houses, they can grow higher and gain dominance, frequently together with large individuals of *Metalasia muricata*. Certain areas of dune strandveld on Grootbos were used for grazing of sheep or cattle in the past. Aerial imagery even shows areas cleared for crops. Grazing

Almost all of the lower slopes of Grootbos and most of the Walker Bay area is characterised by Overberg dune strandveld.

was closely linked to frequent burning for grasses, which would have negatively impacted on the natural vegetation. High cover of grasses and weedy species such as *Pelargonium betulinum* and *Anthospermum aethiopicum* are indicators of too frequent fires in the past.

Agulhas limestone fynbos

Exposed limestone ridges occur all over the lower portion of the reserve. They support three different types of limestone fynbos: A proteoid version, characterised by *Protea obtusifolia*, an ericoid version, characterised by *Erica coccinea* and a restioid version, dominated by *Thamnochortus fraternus*. As they are frequently intermixed and show a variety of transitions they were considered for the purpose of this guide as a single entity: Agulhas limestone fynbos. This vegetation type has recently been classified as vulnerable and is found on the Agulhas Plain where the largest expanses occur between the Klein River lagoon and Grootbos, around Hagelkraal, Heuningrug and Soetanysberg. It is restricted to shallow alkaline bedrock and alkaline grey soils on limestone of the Bredasdorp Formation. On Grootbos this vegetation grows on soils with a pH ranging between 6.9 and 8.1. It is characterised by about two metre high, sparse to medium dense stands of *Protea obtusifolia*, often intermixed with *Leucadendron coniferum* and sometimes with *Leucospermum patersonii*. In some areas, especially on drier slopes where the soil is shallow, *Thamnochortus fraternus* forms dense stands dominating the landscape. Other characteristic species of this vegetation type are *Indigofera brachystachya*, the yellow formed *Erica coccinea*, *Aspalathus forbesii* and the endangered *Cullumia squarrosa*.

A patch of Agulhas limestone fynbos on Grootbos dominated by the pincushion protea,
Leucospermum patersonii.

Overberg sandstone fynbos

Overberg sandstone fynbos is found on approximately 235 hectares of the upper portion of the reserve. The geology is exposed, rocky Table Mountain sandstone. This vegetation has the highest species diversity on Grootbos with an average of 35 species per 50 m^2. It has recently been re-classified as a critically endangered vegetation type owing to the very high number of threatened species. It can be structurally characterised as a low to medium, dense proteoid layer that is usually less than 1.5 m high. There is usually no clear dominance of one species but *Mimetes cucullatus* and *Leucadendron salignum* are the most common, joined by *Aulax umbellata*, *Leucadendron tinctum*, *Leucadendron spissifolium*, *Leucadendron xanthoconus*, *Protea acaulos*, *P. cynaroides*, *P. longifolia* and *P. speciosa*. The most conspicuous among the lower shrubs are *Penaea mucronata* and *Leucospermum prostratum*. The restioid component is variable but *Elegia juncea* in particular can become dominant in places. A number of conspicuous geophytes are found in this vegetation, most notably the showy *Aristea capitata* and *Watsonia stenosiphon*. The large *Bobartia indica* is conspicuous throughout the year, forming extensive stands in some places. Overberg sandstone fynbos is spread irregularly on the lower mountain ranges between Bot River in the west and the Soetanysberg and Bredasdorp in the east.

Above: *Overberg sandstone fynbos on Witkransberg, with the yellow flowering* Euryops abrotanifolius *in the foreground.* Below: *Wetland vegetation on Grootbos.*

Wetland

With the exception of the perennial stream on Witvoetskloof, the catchment areas on Grootbos are not large enough to support permanent streams under the prevailing rainfall regime. In winter some springs can develop, and small rivers may persist until the end of November. As a result, the distribution of true wetlands on the reserve is very limited and only makes up approximately three hectares in total. Despite this small area, the diversity of wetland habitats and associated plant species composition is considerable. Wetland soils are characterised by high organic matter content, their dark colour and a pH between 6.1 and 7.9. The overstorey can be up to 3 m tall and is characterised by *Psoralea arborea*, *Kiggelaria africana*, *Rhus laevigata*, and *Salvia africana-lutea*. The middle layer can be dominated by *Artemesia afra* or by dense stands of the fern *Pteris dentata*.

Leonotis leonurus, *Gunnera perpensa* and *Senecio halimifolius* are also common. The ground layer is extremely variable depending on the moisture availability and includes *Cliffortia ferruginea*, *Helichrysum cymosum*, *Hippia frutescens* and the geophyte *Zantedeschia aethiopica*.

HOW TO USE THIS BOOK

The arrangement of plant families, genera and species in this guide is based on Cape Plants (Manning 2000) with new family circumscriptions as will be appearing in Cape Plants 3 (Manning in prep)*. Where names have recently changed the old name is shown in brackets.

*The ordering of families and genera reflect recent advances in DNA-based studies.

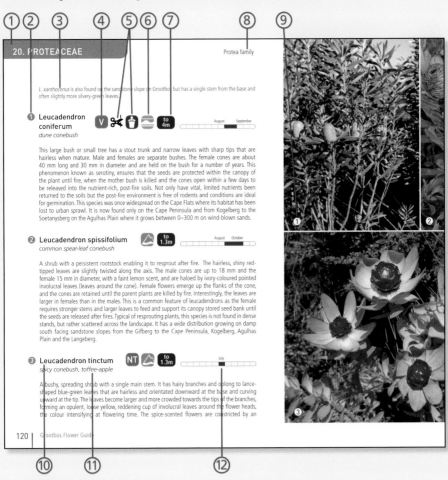

1. Family botanical name.
2. Species number.
3. Species description of other species on Grootbos – not photographed.
4. Red data status-species of conservation concern – see inside flap.
5. Plant uses – see inside flap.
6. Vegetation community where species grows – see inside flap.
7. Height of species.
8. Family common name.
9. Species number on photograph.
10. Species botanical name.
11. Species common name.
12. Flowering months.

A Grootbos sunset over Walker Bay with Cape of Good Hope on the distant horizon.

1. SCHIZAEACEAE

① Schizaea pectinata

 All year

curlygrass or cockscomb fern

A low-growing restio-like fern, with crowded, hairless, thin fronds. The fertile fronds bend into a horizontal terminal brown portion that carries a set of comb-like vertical divisions with sporangia on the inner surface. Often confused as a young restio, the identity of this plant is clearly revealed when the young fronds unfurl in early spring. It is most conspicuous in the first year after fire and is widespread from the Cederberg Mountains to Port Elizabeth and beyond up to Tanzania and Madagascar.

2. ARACEAE

Arum family

② Zantedeschia aethiopica

 June December

arum lily

A stemless, soft herb, with swollen rhizomes and large, stalked heart-shaped leaves that are slimy if crushed. It has the ability to remain evergreen as long as the soil remains damp and prefers shady, wet habitats. The male flowers are arranged on the upper part and the female flowers on the lower half of the yellow spadix, the spathe being snowy white and long lasting. The rhizomes are a favourite food of the porcupines that break up the roots while devouring them, leaving small pieces behind that can grow into new plants. The leaves were traditionally heated and applied as plasters to wounds, sores and boils and also to areas affected by rheumatism and gout. It is most common in the Milkwood forests and wetlands on Grootbos and has a natural distribution throughout South Africa.

> The arum lily frog (2a) often frequents Arum lilies (*Zantedeschia aethiopica*), which it uses as camouflage, feeding on unsuspecting insect visitors. This remarkable little frog is able to effect considerable changes in skin colour over short periods of time. It occurs between the Cape Peninsula and Mossel Bay, but is becoming increasingly rare through destruction of its wetland habitat. Some four years after the completion of the pond in front of Garden Lodge it made its first appearance at Grootbos, 4 km from the closest permanent water body!

3. JUNCAGINACEAE

① Triglochin bulbosa July November

A tufted, rhizomatous perennial that sometimes has fibrous tunics. It has round, green leaves that are visible at flowering time. The flowers are green and fruits are cone shaped and tapering, about 5–10 mm long. The species is restricted to damp, marshy habitats and stretches from the Cape to tropical Africa and the Mediterranean.

4. COLCHICACEAE

Colchicum family

② Baeometra uniflora   August October
beetle lily

A cormous geophyte with 5–8 lance-shaped leaves attached along the stem. It has sessile or short-stalked flowers that face upwards in a group of 1–5. The yellow-orange flowers are unscented and cupped, with a black eye and are reddish on the reverse. This species is pollinated by monkey beetles that eat the pollen (the flowers do not release nectar). It grows on rocky sandstone or granite slopes from Malmesbury to Riversdale.

③ Colchicum eucomoides   July August
men-in-a-boat

A stemless perennial with narrow, tapered leaves that grade into the green, leaf-like bracts. A common species in damp and gravelly open places from Namaqualand to the Eastern Cape. This species was previously a member of the genus *Androcymbium* which, as a result of recent DNA studies, has been included in the genus *Colchicum*. Its concealed flowers are believed to be adapted to pollination by rodents.

Rodent pollination

A number of fynbos species are pollinated by mice. Instead of having showy flowers, rodent pollinated species typically have ground-hugging, dull coloured flowers hidden in the plant. They produce a strong yeasty odour that attracts nocturnal rodents, allowing them to locate the plant's rich source of nectar in the dark, collecting and transferring pollen to other plants in the process.

---

④ Ornithoglossum viride July October
poison onion, slangkop

A cormous geophyte with two or three linear to lance-shaped leaves that are V-shaped and channelled. It has nodding green flowers with maroon margins and filaments thickened below. It is a very poisonous plant that grows on deep sandy soils between Clanwilliam and Riversdale.

We have discovered a total of 41 different orchid species on Grootbos. Of these, eight are species of conservation concern and *Pterygodium vermiferum* is a new species for science first recorded on our reserve. As a visitor to Grootbos there is a good chance that you may never get to see these spectacular flowers in bloom as the majority only flower during the spring after fire. Fortunately Heiner has taken some beautiful pictures that we can share with you at any time of the year – enjoy!

❶ Acrolophia bolusii

   to 80cm  October   December

A robust plant with imbricate leaves up to 300 mm long and 15 mm wide, grading towards the tip into narrow lance-shaped papery sheaths. The flowers are borne on branched stalks that are up to 300 mm long. The flowers are *ca.* 10 mm in diameter, petals and sepals are brownish, lips are dull yellow and often recurved with upcurved margins. This species is found on coastal sandy flats from Hopefield to Bredasdorp, usually below 50 m.

❷ Acrolophia lamellata

 to 50cm   October   November

A species with linear to lance-shaped, keeled, leaves (200 x 15 mm) in a basal fan. The leaves grade into several papery, narrowly lance-shaped cauline sheaths. The inflorescence is usually single, occasionally with several branches, laxly many-flowered. Flowers are at least 15 mm long, with green to purplish-brown sepals and petals. The lip is made up of a white midlobe and purple side lobes. This species is found in coastal sandy areas from Darling to Bredasdorp.

Acrolophia capensis is similar to *A. lamellata* but has smaller flowers, 10–15 mm long, and flowers in December and January.

❸ Acrolophia micrantha

 to 60cm   September   December

Relatively common on Slangkop immediately behind Garden Lodge on Grootbos, this species has imbricate, keeled leaves (300 x 15 mm) with smooth or finely denticulate margins. The upper leaves grade into dry cauline sheaths. The inflorescence is up to 5-branched and laxly, many flowered. The flowers are *ca.* 7 mm in diameter with both sepals and petals being purplish green or brown. The midlobe of the lip is white and the side lobes purplish. It is found predominantly on the coastal forelands from Cape Town to East London.

❹ Bartholina etheliae
spider orchid

 to 23cm   October   December

A slender perennial with a hairy stem and a single, rounded, hairy leaf pressed to the ground. It bears a solitary white flower that has lobed lips with spoon-shaped tips making it look like a spider. It grows between Southern Namibia and the Eastern Cape.

❶ Bonatea speciosa
green wood orchid

This wonderful species was considered by Darwin to be the most 'profoundly modified' of all orchids. Plants are erect and robust with dark green leaves that are oblong to broadly lance-shaped and up to 130 mm long and 40 mm wide. The inflorescences are dense and up to 300 mm long, usually with many green and white flowers up to 90 mm long. The flower spurs are 25–47 mm long and the species is pollinated by hawkmoths. It is found in coastal scrub and forest margins from Yzerfontein to Zimbabwe.

❷ Corycium bicolorum

A robust to slender geophyte with numerous, narrow lance-shaped leaves with broad bases (180 mm x 16 mm). The inflorescences are numerous flowered and dense to 180 mm. The flowers are greenish-yellow with the lateral sepals fused and a 2-lobed lip. The species is found in sandy areas from sea level to 600 m from the Koue Bokkeveld to Mossel Bay and is most profuse following fire.

❸ Corycium carnosum

A slender to fairly robust tuberous geophyte that turns black upon drying. It has narrow lance-shaped leaves (250 x 60 mm) and many flowers in a dense raceme. The flowers and sepals are green and the petals pink with a whitish-pink lip. The lip has two broad diverging lobes. It flowers after fires and occurs mostly in sandstone seeps from Cape Peninsula to Port Elizabeth.

❹ Corycium excisum

A slender to fairly robust tuberous geophyte that turns black upon drying. It has many linear leaves and lime-green flowers in a dense raceme. The lateral sepals are fused. This species is rare and found on sandy flats from Piketberg to Agulhas from sea level to 300 m. It only flowers after fire.

❺ Corycium orobanchoides

A slender or robust tuberous geophyte with many lance-shaped leaves that are characteristically barred with red below. Its many, rather unpleasantly scented flowers are in dense racemes (5 x 15 mm) and are yellow-green with purple apices to the petals and fused lateral sepals. It grows on sandy flats from sea level to 500 m from Klawer to Albertinia. It is a common species often growing as a weed alongside roadsides or in lawns!

❶ Disa bracteata

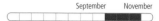

September   November

A geophyte with linear to lance-shaped leaves and many flowers in a dense raceme. The flowers are green with maroon tinted sepals and pendant spurs (3–4.5 mm long). The flowers have shortly overtopping bracts with tapering tips. This species is widespread and common in the fynbos region, especially in areas of mild disturbance. In undisturbed vegetation it is widespread, but less common. It is a roadside weed in Australia following accidental introduction from South Africa. The species is self-pollinated and readily sets seed, enabling it to colonise new habitats fairly rapidly.

❷ Disa cornuta

February   September to

A robust plant with densely overlapping leaves reaching the base of the flowerhead. The species has numerous flowers that have bracts as tall as or overtopping the flowers. The flowers face downwards and are purple and silvery-green. This species is widespread and locally common from the West Coast through the Eastern Cape into Zimbabwe. It is one of the very few orchids that occur in both the winter- and summer-rainfall areas.

❸ Disa densiflora

October

A slender, tuberous geophyte with linear to lance-shaped leaves that overlap each other. Its flowers are in dense, slender racemes. The petals and lip are dull green, while the sepals are rusty red to green, and the 2–3 mm long spur is constricted at the base. It grows on sandy soils from the Cape Peninsula to Bredasdorp with an outlying population at the Storms River mouth.

❹ Disa hallackii

October   November

A robust tuberous geophyte with lance-shaped leaves scattered along the stem. The flowers have prominent bracts, green sepals and purplish petals. The spur is 5 mm long. This species is very rare along the coast on sandstone slopes from the Cape Peninsula to Port Elizabeth. The known populations near Cape Town and Port Elizabeth appear to have become extinct and until the species was discovered on Grootbos and neighbouring Flower Valley in November 2002 the only other known population was in the Mossel Bay area. This species is one of the most threatened South African orchid species.

① Disa purpurascens
bloumoederkappie

October November

A slender tuberous geophyte with approximately 10 basal, linear (to 1 mm broad) leaves. At the time of flowering the leaves are dry. It has a few (1–7) blue to violet-purple flowers with green ends to the petals and a dark purple lip. It has a conical spur and an upcurved lip. This species is uncommon, growing in well-drained, rocky areas in full sunlight from sea level to 300 m from the Cape Peninsula to Port Elizabeth.

Disa graminifolia, also recorded on Grootbos, is similar to *Disa purpurascens* but with elliptic spur and lip margin down-curved.

② Disa reticulata

November December

Plants with linear to lance-shaped leaves up to 150 mm long. The inflorescence is cylindrical, dense with numerous flowers (30–150 mm long) with bracts reaching to the tops of the flowers. Flowers have a soapy smell and are lime green, occasionally with some maroon tinting or mottling on the petals or sepals. This species is rare within its distribution range in seasonally damp places between sea level and 1 700 m from the Cape Peninsula to Knysna. It is most common after fire.

③ Disperis capensis
moederkappie

July September

A tuberous geophyte with a softly hairy stem and two lance-shaped suberect leaves. It has a single green and magenta or cream flower with darker margins, conspicuously tailed sepals and a lip limb that curves downwards. This species is widespread in the fynbos region growing from the Pakhuis Pass in the northern Cederberg to Grahamstown. This species provides no floral reward to pollinators, instead tricking the pollen-collecting bee *Xylocopa rufitarus* through mimicking flowers of Polygala species.

④ Disperis villosa

August September

A tuberous geophyte with short hairs on its stem. It has two alternate, elliptic leaves and 1–3 flowered inflorescences. The flowers are greenish-yellow and have a strong sweet scent. The middle sepal has a deep sac-like, pubescent hood projecting horizontally. This species is common in the Western Cape where it is found growing mainly on clay soils from Clanwilliam to Mossel Bay with a single record from Port Elizabeth.

① Eulophia aculeata

January · · · · · · · · · November to

A rhizomatous geophyte with linear to lance-shaped, stiffly erect, pleated leaves that are partly to fully developed by flowering time. The dull ivory, to white flowers are few to many (3–27 flowered) in a dense inflorescence and without spurs. This species is found from the Cape Peninsula to Mpumalanga.

② Eulophia litoralis
harlequin orchid

January · · · · · · · · · November to

A rhizomatous geophyte with leaves absent or poorly developed, rarely a single leaf up to 20 mm. The flowering stem is 220–660 mm tall and the inflorescence is elongated and lax with 6–27 flowers. The flower sepals are yellowish-green, while the petals and lip are yellow and the side lobes tinged purple. This is a rare species confined to a narrow belt along the coast between the Cape Flats and Plettenberg Bay in sandy soils.

③ Holothrix cernua

January · · · · · · July to

A slender, tuberous geophyte with leaves generally withered at flowering time. The flowers are on scapes (90–240 mm high) without bracts and with long reflexed rough hairs. The flowers have densely hairy sepals and petals that are entire and cream to lime-green in colour. This species is frequent in sandy or stony places from Vanrhynsdorp to Grahamstown, generally flowering only after fire.

④ Holothrix exilis

March · · · · · October to

A slender, tuberous geophyte that has a flowering stem with long fine hairs. It has two smooth, basal, oval shaped leaves and has few (to many) green flowers in a dense raceme. The petals and lip are entire and it has a slightly curved spur. It has been recorded on the Cape Peninsula and from Riversdale to the Kei River in the Eastern Cape. The discovery of this species on Grootbos was the first time it had been recorded on the Agulhas Plain.

⑤ Holothrix schlechteriana

February · · · · · · · October to

A slender tuberous geophyte with a thinly, velvety hairy flowering stem and two basal, hairless, oval shaped leaves. It has many flowers in a dense raceme. The flowers have green sepals and petals and the lip is either green or yellow. The petals have 4–9 thread-like lobes and the lip is spurred and divided into 5–11 thread-like lobes. The species grows from Namaqualand to the Eastern Cape.

Another three Holothrix species have been recorded on Grootbos. *Holothrix grandiflora* is found in rock crevices and has two oval-shaped leaves that often wither at flowering, and flowers with a white lip with pale green or lilac base, *H. mundii*, has two fleshy oval basal leaves, flowers in a condensed raceme with green sepals and white petals and lip, *H. villosa* has two hairy basal leaves and the flower lip is spurred and with 3–5 lobes.

❶ Pterygodium acutifolium

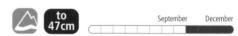

September   December

A slender tuberous geophyte with 3–4 oblong-shaped leaves spaced up the stem and a few flowers (1–14) in a lax raceme. The flower's sepals are lime green and the petals and lip are yellow. This species is common and widespread, flowering mostly after fire and is found in marshes and seeps in fynbos vegetation from Piketberg to Port Elizabeth. The species is superficially similar to *Pterygoidium catholicum* (see below), but is found in wetter habitats, the flower colour is generally a richer butter-yellow and older flowers do not turn red as in *P. catholicum*.

❷ Pterygodium caffrum

September November

A slender tuberous geophyte with oval to lance-shaped leaves spaced up the stem. It has many flowers in a dense raceme (28 x 15 mm). The flowers have pale greenish sepals and yellow lip and petals. The lip has two broad lobes. This species is locally common from Ceres to Knysna with a single record from Port Elizabeth. It grows in low fynbos from near sea level to 450 m.

❸ Pterygodium catholicum
cowled friar

September November

A slender tuberous geophyte with 2–4 oblong to lance-shaped leaves spaced up the stem and 1–14 yellowish-green flowers, often flushed red, in a lax flower head. The flowers have a strong and pungent scent. A common species in renosterveld and fynbos throughout the Cape Floristic Region. The species often forms dense colonies and is thought to multiply vegetatively.

❹ Pterygodium cruciferum

September November

A slender tuberous geophyte with 2–3 linear to elliptic shaped leaves (190 x 18 mm). The flower heads have 2–6 yellowish green flowers. The appendage inside the flower has a crucifix shape, hence the specific name *P. cruciferum*. This species is very rare, growing in fynbos from sea level to 100 m from Mamre up the West Coast to the Bredasdorp vicinity. Prior to our discovery of this species on Grootbos, it was only known from one locality on the Cape Flats, one in Darling and one locality near Cape Agulhas.

❶ Pterygodium vermiferum

August   October

One of the new species discovered on Grootbos, *P. vermiferum* was first recorded on Grootbos on the path up to Swartkransberg at an altitude of 385 m by Heiner Lutzeyer in 2003. Subsequent collections have been made on these western slopes of the mountain at three separate sites about 260 m apart. A second population is located along the road between Stanford and Gansbaai and a third population is at Die Kelders at an altitude of 50 m. The total known area of extent of this species measures just 5.5 by 3.0 km along an L-shaped range, the majority of which is conserved within the Grootbos Reserve!

This is a small, slender tuberous geophyte with a highly specialised, very large lip appendage that secretes oil and is intimately connected to pollination by female oil-collecting bees in the genus Rediviva (Hymenoptera: Mellittidae). In addition to the unusual floral structures this species is adapted for pollination by autonomous selfing (self-pollination). Within a day of the flower opening, the loosely aggregated pollen grains tumble out of the gaping slits that run along the length of the pollen-forming sacs and adhere to the nearest lobes of the female stigma within the same flower. The flowers wither within three days and set copious quantities of seeds without the intervention of a pollinator. The species is named vermiferum on account of the extraordinary, wormlike outgrowths of the rostellum (this is a specialised sterile organ that usually acts to separate the male and female parts of the flower to prevent self-pollination), vermes = worm, ferus = bearing.

The species flowers most profusely after fire. A survey in October 2007 of the Swartkransberg population revealed that the number of flowering plants was considerably reduced, to 20–30% of the plants counted in the previous year following the 2006 fire. The non-flowering plants were represented by just a single basal leaf.

❷ Pterygodium volucris

September   October

A slender geophyte with 3–4 oval to oblong leaves to 140 x 50 mm. The inflorescence is cylinder-shaped and up to 150 mm long with many flowers. The flowers have green sepals and lime petals and lips and are strongly scented. The flower bracts are oval to lance shaped, acute and curved downwards. This species is often recorded under bushes and is widespread in the western and southern parts of the Cape Floristic Region from Clanwilliam to Humansdorp.

❸ Satyrium bicorne

September   October

An erect geophyte with two (seldom one) oval to round leaves growing on the ground. The inflorescence has between 4–40 pale greenish yellow flowers that are faintly to darkly tinged purple-brown. The flower bracts have fine hairs on the edges and are curved downwards. The flowers produce a spicy fragrance in the evening in order to attract moth pollinators. It is common in sandy soils from sea level to 1 200 m from Namaqualand to the Eastern Cape. It flowers mainly after fires and has been found to be pollinated by settling moths.

❶ Satyrium bicallosum

October November

An erect geophyte, with between one and three partly spreading, oval-shaped leaves situated near the soil surface. The inflorescence is elongated with between 6–150 dull-white, faintly greenish flowers with a pale purple patch up the spurs. This species is locally common from Clanwilliam to the Cape Peninsula and eastwards to George. It grows on dry to damp sandy soils and usually is found singly or in small groups, flowering after fire.

Mistaken for a mushroom

The tiny white flowers of *Satyrium bicallosum* release a delicate smell reminiscent of mushrooms. This attracts a minute fungus gnat known as Sciara, which usually lays its eggs in mushrooms. Tricked by the flower, the gnat crawls inside, touches the sexual organs, tiny pollen packets become glued to its thorax, and it acts as the orchid's pollinator.

❷ Satyrium carneum
rooikoppie, rooi trewwa

September November

A robust ground orchid, with stout stems arising from two lobed tubers that are joined at the top. It has 2–4 thick, fleshy green leaves, the lowest two being partly pressed onto the ground. The unscented, strongly hooded pink (very occasionally white) inflorescence is stout with between 19–38 flowers. They are visited by sunbirds. This species occurs between the Cape Peninsula and Stilbaai in dune bush

The leaves of *Satyrium carneum* encircle the stem and often fill up with water thereby forming a moat around the flower that effectively prevents ants and other nectar thieves from reaching the flower.

vegetation, in fynbos on coastal hills and on ridges on moist to dry sands and limestones. It is restricted to the coastal belt between sea level and 300 m and is threatened by harvesting for horticultural purposes, urbanisation, alien plants and agriculture. From experience with search and rescue of this species we have found that it transplants well if harvested between October and December when it is in a dormant state and the dried leaves are still visible. It must be replanted in suitable alkaline sandy habitat by the end of the following April as it does not survive the winter in storage.

❸ Satyrium coriifolium
ewwa trewwa

August October

A robust ground orchid with stout stems and 2–4 leathery, oval to elliptic pointed leaves. The leaves are erect to spreading and purple-spotted towards the sheathing leaf bases. The

unscented flowers are bright yellow to bright orange, often with a red tinged lip. They are pollinated by sunbirds. It is a locally frequent species in sandy, moist open flats from the Cederberg Mountains to the Cape Peninsula and eastwards to Port Elizabeth. In some places it has become established as a roadside weed.

1 Satyrium lupulinum

to 30cm

September   October

A slender to stout tuberous geophyte with 1–3 leaves spreading near the ground. The longest leaf is oval-shaped, 20–80 mm long and often with a purple underside. The inflorescence is rather dense with between 12–20 dull yellowish green, purple tinged flowers. Occasional after fire from the Cape Peninsula to Port Elizabeth.

2 Satyrium odorum
soet trewwa

to 55cm

August   October

A robust, leafy geophyte with 2–6 narrow oval leaves scattered along the stem. It has a few to many yellow flowers with a purple tinge in a moderately dense raceme. The flowers have spurs that are between 13–18 mm long. Found in partly shady, humus-rich soils near trees and bushes from sea level to 650 m from Saldanha to Riversdale.

Other Satyrium species recorded on Grootbos are *S. bracteatum*, which has flowers that are dull white or yellow with dark reddish brown markings and no spurs, and *S. ligulatum* that has its leaves clustered near the base of the stem and has many yellowish green to dull creamy white flowers.

3 Empodium plicatum
ploegtydblommetjie

to 20cm

April   June

A cormous geophyte with pale basal sheath. It has 1–4, narrow leaves that are surrounded at the base by pale sheaths, sometimes absent or just emerging at flowering time and widening later. The leaves are spreading and deeply pleated with hairy ribs beneath. The flowers are yellow, and borne at ground level with the ovary enclosed by the sheaths and drawn into an elongated beak up to 100 mm long. It grows on slopes from the Bokkeveld Mountains to Bredasdorp.

❶ Spiloxene capensis
peacock flower

July — October

A cormous geophyte with several spreading leaves, keeled and V-shaped in cross-section. It has yellow or white flowers that are variable in size and occur singly per flowering stem. The flower centre is iridescent blue or green, banded on the reverse (occasionally dark and non-iridescent). The flowers have a long solitary bract that is sheath-like. It grows in seasonally wet areas between Clanwilliam and Oudtshoorn.

Spiloxene capensis counts amongst the most striking of Ultra-violet-marked flowers. Human's and insect's versions of sight have evolved independently from one another. While human's primary colours are red, green and blue, the majority of day-flying insect's primary colours are yellow, blue and ultra-violet. As such insects see *Spiloxene capensis* as a purple flower with a red centre.

7. TECOPHILAEACEAE

Cyanella family

❷ Cyanella hyacinthoides
lady's-hand, raaptoluintjie

August — November

A perennial with narrow, lance-shaped leaves that are sometimes velvety and grow in a basal rosette. The leaf margins are wavy to very crisped. It bears unscented or fragrant mauve (occasionally white) flowers on spreading flower heads, with five upper and 1 lower stamen. It is mostly found on clay and granite slopes, often in renosterveld from Namaqualand in the north to Riversdale in the south.

❸ Cyanella lutea
five-fingers, lady's hand,
geelraaptol

September — October

A perennial with 4–6 lance-shaped leaves in a basal rosette, up to 15 cm and ribbed with wavy margins. The leaves have usually withered by the time of flowering. It bears many golden-yellow, markedly veined, fragrant flowers on a branched flowering stalk. In some areas like Namaqualand the uintjies (corms) are considered to be a high-quality staple food. Harvesting occurs in the wet season (July to October) and the corms are eaten raw or are roasted or boiled in milk. This species was also used traditionally together with *Lobostemon fruticosus* (agtdaegeneesbossie) to make an ointment used for sores. This is a widespread species of both winter and summer rainfall areas.

❶ Aristea africana

maagbossie

January ... October to

A small, evergreen, usually branched perennial with flattened stems and linear leaves that are 1.5–4 mm wide. The flowers are blue, tepals mostly 8–12 mm long, with spathes that are translucent with dark keels, finely fringed and sometimes rusty brown at the tips. This species is widespread, growing from Gifberg to Bredasdorp and Riversdale.

❷ Aristea capitata

blouvuurpyl

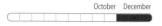
October December

A large and robust, clump-forming perennial with strap-like fibrous leaves (much like those of a Watsonia). It has tall, cylindrical stems that are closely branched at the tip so that the flower clusters are crowded and overlapping. The spathes are dry, membranous and translucent with dark keels. It is easy to identify as it is the only large Aristea on Grootbos and grows on the upper sandstone slopes in moist areas. It is a popular garden plant that does not transplant easily. It grows naturally on damp mountain slopes between Piketberg and George.

❸ Aristea glauca

October December

An evergreen, rhizomatous plant that forms low cushions, spreading by stolons. The stems are strongly compressed and two-winged, either branched or unbranched. The leaves are narrow, 1–3 mm wide, smooth and linear. The flowers are blue, about 18 mm long and the spathes and bracts are green to brown with wide translucent margins. It is a species of lower slopes that grows from the Cape Peninsula inland to Ceres and eastwards to Riversdale.

❹ Aristea spiralis

September December

A perennial that is usually branched and can be differentiated from other Aristeas on Grootbos on the basis of its large white or pale blue flowers with a small dark eye, facing to the side. It has flattened 2-winged stems and fairly broad, soft leaves that are 4–7 mm wide. The sessile flowers face to the side and produce long, cylindrical fruits. The spathes are green with transparent margins. It grows on rocky sandstone slopes up to 600 m from the Cape Peninsula to Knysna and only flowers after fire.

Another two species of Aristea have been recorded on Grootbos, *A. bakeri* (*macrocarpa*), which grows to 1 m tall and has sword shaped fibrous leaves that are up to 20 mm wide, and *A. oligocephala*, which is 15–25 cm high, has dichotomously branching compressed stems, and spathes and bracts that are silvery translucent with narrow dark keels.

❶ Babiana nana

August   September

A dwarf perennial with soft textured, soft-haired leaves that are short, broad and ribbed. It bears large, fragrant, 2-lipped, blue or violet flowers with white markings on the lower tepals. The flower tube is 12–17 mm long, the inner bracts are forked at the tip and the ovary is hairless. It grows on sandy coastal flats and dunes from Lamberts Bay to Mossel Bay.

❷ Babiana tubiflora

September   October

A plant with underground stems and hairy, pleated, linear to lance-shaped leaves. The flowers are white to cream, sometimes with red markings, and the flower tube is 55–85 mm long. It occurs on sandy flats near the sea from Elands Bay to Riversdale.

Babiana ambigua has netted corm tunics, linear to lance-shaped leaves that are longer than the stem and blue to mauve flowers with white markings. It is also found in Overberg dune strandveld.

❸ Bobartia indica

   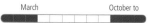

March   October to

An evergreen, rhizomatous plant that looks somewhat like a restio without bracts. It has terete leaves that are trailing and longer than the stems. The bright yellow flowers are enclosed by green spathes arranged in dense flowerheads of 4–40 bundles per stem. On Grootbos it is found on the rocky upper sandstone slopes, and has a natural distribution from Mamre on the West Coast to Caledon in the Overberg.

❹ Chasmanthe aethiopica
cobralily, suurkanolpypie

April   July

An unbranched, sturdy cormous geophyte with several firm sword-shaped, ribbed leaves in a fan that are present at flowering time. The flower spike has many 22 mm long, stalkless orange flowers arranged in a flat plane. The uppermost tepals extend about three times longer than the lower. This species is pollinated by sunbirds and its bright orange seeds have a juicy covering that are eaten and dispersed by birds. It is common on the edge of the Grootbos Milkwood forests, and has a natural distribution on coastal hills from Darling to the Eastern Cape.

❺ Ferraria crispa
spinnekopblom, uiltjie

July   October

A cormous geophyte with fleshy, broad, overlapping leaves that partly conceal the branched, straight or slightly twisted stem. The flowers, which are about 35 mm across, are carrion-scented to attract flies and are open for only one day. It grows on sandy soils from Clanwilliam to Willowmore and along the coast from Kleinmond to Mossel Bay.

① Geissorhiza aspera
sysie

August September

A perennial with a finely velvety stem and sword-shaped leaves that have thickened margins and midribs. The blue to violet flowers have a very short tube (1–2 mm long) and one stamen that is slightly shorter than the others. The bracts are dry and brown in the upper half. This is a widespread and common species of sandy soils from the Gifberg to Cape Agulhas.

② Gladiolus brevifolius
March pypie, Autumn pipes

March April

The flowering stem bears short, largely or entirely sheathing leaves on the stem. The flowers are small, 30–40 mm long, with a dorsal tepal 20–29 mm long and a perianth tube 11–13 mm long. The flowers range from deep to pale pink, or cream to mauve, the lower tepals usually with a yellow transverse to obscure median band edged in darker pink, or with a median dark streak when the tepals are pale coloured. This species is unscented on Grootbos. It grows naturally from Piketberg to Agulhas.

③ Gladiolus carinatus
sandpypie, blue Afrikaner

June mid-September

This species is readily recognised by its three foliage leaves with thickened midribs. It bears large, extremely sweet-scented blue, yellow or occasionally pink flowers that are marked with yellow and blue on the lower tepals and have a short tube, 6–10 mm long. The base of the flowering stem is distinctively purple mottled. This species grows on deep coastal sands and lower slopes from Namaquland to Knysna.

④ Gladiolus carneus
painted lady, white Afrikaner

October November

A geophyte with narrow sword-shaped leaves that can usually be recognised by its large, funnel-shaped pale pink or white flowers, often with dark pink linear to spear-shaped markings on the lower tepals. It grows on sandstone slopes, often in damp sites from the Cape Peninsula to Outeniqua Mountains.

⑤ Gladiolus cunonius
lepelblom, spoon flower

September November

The very peculiar structure of the flower of this species makes it easy to identify. The dorsal tepal is elongate, 26–29 mm long, and strongly concave giving rise to the plant's common name lepelblom (spoon flower). It has soft-textured, narrowly sword-shaped leaves and is a coastal species that grows between Saldanha Bay and Knysna.

❶ Gladiolus debilis
little painted lady

One of the loveliest species of Gladiolus, recognised by its fairly large white flowers. The lower tepals are characterised by their distinctive red markings. These include chevrons, diamonds or streaks and lines in very regular patterns. The base of the throat is also marked with a circle of red. It grows on sandstone slopes from Bainskloof to the Cape Peninsula and Bredasdorp.

❷ Gladiolus maculatus
brown Afrikaner

A slender perennial geophyte with narrow, leathery, short-bladed leaves. It bears scented, moderately large, funnel-shaped flowers, typically with tan or dark brown shading and mottling on a pale background. Edges of the upper tepals are transparent. Flowers are scented during day and night. It grows on clay slopes, mainly in renosterveld from the Cape Peninsula to the Eastern Cape.

❸ Gladiolus martleyi
basterherfspypie

A small flowered, autumn-blooming Gladiolus. The flowering stem bears two or three short sheathing leaves. The sweetly fragrant flowers are usually pale to deep pink or occasionally lilac to mauve, and have strongly marked nectar guides on the lower tepals consisting of transverse bands or spear-shaped yellow marks edged with dark pink or purple. It is similar to *G. brevifolius*, although that species seldom has such strongly differentiated nectar guides and rarely has scented flowers. It grows on sandy and rocky flats and lower slopes from the Bokkeveld escarpment to Albertinia.

❹ Gladiolus meridionalis

The pink flowers of this species are adapted to pollination by sunbirds and have a long perianth tube with a wide cylindrical upper part and large quantities of nectar. Somewhat unusual for sunbird pollination, the nectar has a relatively high sugar concentration and is sucrose dominant. Plants have three leaves, the leaf blades are slightly fleshy and without thickened margins or a visible midrib. They grow in stony sandstone soils in low fynbos on mountain slopes and flats from Gansbaai to Elim with an outlying population in the Port Elizabeth district.

❺ Gladiolus miniatus

Unmistakeable with its salmon-orange perianth, usually with darker colourings on the midlines of the tepals. The shape of the flower, together with its colour suggests that it is pollinated

by sunbirds. The flowers produce copious amounts of nectar (>10 microlitres/flower). It has a tight fan of short, narrowly lance-shaped, firm leaves and distinctive corm tunics of coarse fibres. These accumulate with age into a dense mass of coarse fibres that form a thick neck around the base of the stem. A rare endemic of the limestone outcrops along the south coast from Hawston to Riversdale. This species always grows near the seashore in sight of the ocean.

❶ Gladiolus overbergensis

July   September

Plants with a globose corm with coarsely fibrous tunics and sword-shaped to linear leaves that are rough and scabrid. It has beautiful red to orange flowers in a 2–5-flowered, erect spike. It is a rare species that is only observed in the first year following fire. A very localised species, restricted to the Agulhas Plain most notably between Stanford and Elim. It is thought to be pollinated by sunbirds. This species had never been recorded on Grootbos until the spring following the 2006 fire when it bloomed in profusion on the upper sandstone slopes of the reserve. Having made a spectacular appearance for one season it has once again gone dormant awaiting the next fire.

❷ Gladiolus vaginatus

February   April

A plant with two leathery leaves, 1–1.5 mm wide, without visible veins. It has fragrant blue to grey flowers, mostly in a 2–6-flowered spike, with dark streaks on the lower tepals. The flower tube is 6.5–20 mm long. This species grows on limestone and clay-loam (in renosterveld) from the Cape Peninsula to Knysna.

❸ Gladiolus variegatus

September   October

A beautiful species characteristic of the limestone outcrops in the area. It only grows between Grootbos and Cape Agulhas on limestone outcrops. It has a globose corm with woody to coarse fibrous tunics. The leaves are linear and have a thickened midrib. The flowers are white with the lower tepals having irregular red spots. The flowers are in one- to four-flowered spikes.

Gladiolus rogersii is a classic example of a 'windsock-flower'. It has a thin flexible flowering stem that enables it to turn its 'back' on rainy weather and protect its pollen from moisture, enabling the flower to stay open at night or when it rains.

Gladiolus rogersii has 3–6, more or less bell-like blue to purple flowers with yellow or white transverse markings on the lower tepals.

❶ Hesperantha falcata
aandblom

July   October

A geophyte with a bell-shaped corm that has a flat base and smooth tunics. It has three to five sword-shaped leaves. The flowers are white or yellow with the outer tepals being red to brown on the outside. There are 3–8 flowers per spike. The white-flowered plants are sweetly fragrant in the late afternoon and evening; while the yellow flowered ones open during the middle of the day and are unscented, suggesting different pollinators visit the different coloured flowers. A widespread species on sandstone, shale and coastal flats from Gifberg to Port Elizabeth.

❷ Hesperantha radiata

August   October

A geophyte with an obliquely flattened corm with overlapping tunics. It has short, linear, fleshy leaves and many nodding white to cream flowers that are sweetly scented and open after sunset. A widespread species on sandstone, granite and clay soils from Namaqualand to Swaziland.

❸ Ixia flexuosa

August   September

A geophyte with a wiry, often unbranched stem. The leaves are linear to sword-shaped. The flowers are mostly 4–12 per spike, congested, pink, mauve, or white with darker streaks and a slight musky odour. The flower tube is 4–6 mm long and the stamens are fully exerted. It is found mostly on clay slopes from the Cape Peninsula to Riversdale.

❹ Ixia odorata

September   November

A geophyte with linear to lance-shaped leaves that are often loosely coiled above. The sweetly fragrant, pale yellow or cream flowers are crowded in spikes of 5–12. The flower tube is narrowly funnel-shaped and 5–11 mm long. It has been recorded on sandstone and granite slopes between Citrusdal and Grootbos. Prior to its discovery on Grootbos this species had not been recorded eastwards of Hermanus.

❺ Ixia orientalis

September   October

A geophyte with stems that sometimes have one to three small branchlets. The leaves are linear and only 1.5–5 mm long. The flowers are cream to mauve-pink and fairly crowded in groups of 5–10 per spike. They have narrow, funnel-shaped flower tubes that are 7–10 mm long with filaments protruding. It grows on flats between Villiersdorp and Port Alfred.

Two other Ixias have been recorded on Grootbos, *Ixia dubia* which has crowded, orange to yellow flowers with dark centres and *Ixia polystachya* with white to pink or mauve flowers often with a dark centre.

① Melasphaerula ramosa

fairy bells

September   October

A beautiful, delicate plant with a bell-shaped corm that grows in the shade of the Milkwood forests on Grootbos. The small cream to pale yellow flowers are many in a lax, compound spike. They have a dark streak down the middle. The flowers are probably pollinated by small flies attracted by the sour, musk-like odour. It is the only species within its genus and is widespread between southern Namibia and the Swartberg Mountains in sheltered, damp places among rocks and on the edge of thickets. It has potential as a horticultural plant.

② Moraea bituminosa

October   December

A geophyte with a corm of between 15–20 mm in diameter, with dark brown tunics, the inner layers unbroken and the outer irregularly fragmented. It has two linear, channelled leaves that are sometimes twisted. They are trailing on the ground, usually longer than the stem. The lower leaf is basal and the upper attached to the lowest aerial node. It has a branched and sticky stem. The flowers are bright yellow (rarely purple) with deep yellow nectar guides on the outer tepals. The flowers open at midday and fade in the late afternoon. This species is native to the higher rainfall areas of the south-western Cape where it is common on flats and slopes with sandstone-derived soils between Wellington and Bredasdorp.

③ Moraea fugax

hottentotsbrood

August   October

A geophyte with a pale fibrous corm, 15–30 mm in diameter. It has one or two channelled leaves that are attached to the flowering stem well above the ground, immediately below the first branch. The leaves are trailing and longer than the stem, occasionally loosely twisted at the end. The flowering stem is erect to slightly declining with a conspicuous, long lower internode. The flowers are white, blue or yellow and

> The edible corms of *Moraea fugax* were an important food source for early human inhabitants of the Cape. The corm tunics are abundant in caves and shelters. Today the corms are occasionally eaten as a curiosity by humans but they remain a favourite of mole rats, baboons and porcupines.

strongly scented. They open at midday and fade towards sunset. This species has a wide distribution range extending from Namaqualand to the southern Cape.

④ Moraea lewisiae

October   December

A geophyte with two or three linear, channelled, flat or twisting leaves. The fragrant yellow flowers are borne in lateral clusters and are speckled with black in the centre. They are enclosed

by green spathes and have six equal tepals that are 19–24 mm long. This species is characterised by an exceptional style that is divided into 6 threadlike branches. It occurs in varying habitats, mostly dry sites, from Namaqualand to Humansdorp.

1 Moraea longistyla

A yellow or salmon-flowered Moraea with its stem flexed outward above the leaf sheath and corm with a tunic of black wiry fibres. It has a single, linear, channelled leaf that is trailing above. The flowers are enclosed in a green spathe and the tepals are unequal in length, 25–35 mm long. A species predominately found in clay soils from Ceres to Caledon.

2 Moraea miniata
pronktulp

Fairly common in coastal dune soils on Grootbos, *M. miniata* has salmon flowers that are minutely speckled in the centre and enclosed in a sticky spathe. The corm is covered with a tunic of black fibres. It has two or three linear, channelled, trailing leaves. This species is usually found on clay slopes from Namaqualand to Riverdale and the Karoo.

3 Moraea papilionacea

A small plant with corms of 5–15 mm in diameter that have brown to black tunics. It has between 2–4 linear leaves, with slightly ciliate margins, that are up to 7 mm wide and occasionally longer than the flowering stem. The stem is lightly hairy, 1–2 internodes long and up to 5-branched, mainly from the base but sometimes also from the upper node. The sweetly-scented flowers are salmon pink or pale yellow, with yellow nectar guides on the outer tepals outlined in yellow, green or red. It grows from the Cederberg Mountains to Bredasdorp on a variety of soils from poorly-drained sands to seasonally damp clays.

4 Moraea pyrophila

A species that only flowers in the late summer within weeks of a fire. On Grootbos we only recorded this species in the month after the February 2006 fire and have not seen it since. It has pale yellow flowers, enclosed in green spathes. Its stem flexes outward above the leaf sheath. It has a single, linear, channelled, spine-tipped rigid leaf inserted high up on the stem. The corm is covered in a tunic of wiry, black fibres. It occurs on sandstone slopes between Piketberg and Bredasdorp.

❶ Moraea ramosissima

October   December

The largest Moraea on Grootbos, this species is much branched and has several linear, channelled, shiny leaves in a two-ranked fan. The flowers are yellow with darker yellow nectar guides on the outer tepals. The tepals are unequal in length, the outer being larger than the inner. It has spiny roots to deter moles and the corm is covered with brown, cartilaginous tunics. It grows on damp sandy or stony flats and slopes between Gifberg and the Eastern Cape and mainly flowers after fire.

Moraea ramosissima relies on molerats to disperse their bulbs. Its main bulb is protected by a cage of thorny roots, outside of which are masses of minute bulbs. When the molerat attempts to get to the main bulbs it dislodges the small bulbs, dispersing them through the mole's burrow system.

❷ Moraea setifolia

September   November

A plant with corms covered in pale, soft tunic fibres. It has one or two linear, channelled leaves that trail above. The flowers are enclosed in translucent spathes and are small, pale mauve with orange and white nectar guides. The outer tepals are 12–18 mm long. It occurs on sandy and gravelly flats and slopes from Namaqualand to Grahamstown.

❸ Moraea tripetala

August   December

A slender geophyte with one narrow leaf, longer than the stem (usually unbranched). The flowers are pale mauve to deep violet and have three large outer tepals that are bearded within. The other three tepals are minute, hence the Latin name tripetala. It is widespread and common on flats and slopes from Nieuwoudtville to George.

❹ Moraea viscaria

September   December

This Moraea is characterised by its sticky stems and white flowers that are brownish below, fragrant and open in the late afternoon. It has brown corm tunics that are gnarled, woody to coarse fibrous and layered. The 2–3, linear, channelled leaves trail above. It is found on sandy flats from Saldanha Bay to Cape Agulhas.

The fynbos is full of thieving insects that bite through the sides of flowers and steal the nectar without doing the pollinating. So many flowers have developed advanced security devices in order to safeguard their nectar for the genuine pollinators. One of the most effective means of thwarting the nectar thieves is through having sticky coatings on flowers or stems such as in *Moraea viscaria*. This prevents ants and other insects from climbing into the flower and gums up the mouthpieces of bees.

Other Moraea species on Grootbos are the large yellow flowered, unbranched *Moraea angusta*, the 1 m tall non-sticky, hairless, sturdy *M. bellendenii* of sandy places, *M. bulbillifera*, which also occurs in coastal soils and produces cormlets at each node, the slightly scented yellow or salmon flowering *M. collina*, which has flowers enclosed in gray spathes, *M. neglecta* with sticky nodes and yellow flowers with darkly stippled markings on the outer tepals and *M. virgata* with its sessile lateral, unscented flower clusters.

① Romulea dichotoma

to 35cm   September   October

A geophyte with two or three 4-grooved leaves, sometimes minutely hairy, the lowest one being basal. The flowers are pink with a yellowish cup, tepals elliptical and 16–32 mm long. It is restricted to coastal sands from Stanford to Humansdorp.

② Romulea obscura

to 15cm   August   October

A geophyte with a corm rounded at its base. It has 3–6 leaves basal or some clasping the stem. The leaves are narrowly four-grooved, 0.5–1 mm in diameter. The flowers are yellow or apricot to red, often with dark blotches around the greenish to yellow cup. The tepals are 10–40 mm long. It occurs on sandy flats from Clanwilliam to Cape Agulhas.

③ Romulea rosea
froetang

  to 15cm   July   November

A stemless geophyte with 3–6 threadlike, rather stiff hairless leaves that are up to 36 cm long. The flower stalks are 30–80 mm long and the pale lilac-pink or sometimes white flowers have a dark zone above the yellow cup. The outside of the tepal lobes are yellowish-green and dark striped. It is common on sandy flats, especially disturbed places, from Nieuwoudtville to Port Elizabeth.

Another two species are found on Grootbos, *Romulea flava* with a single basal threadlike leaf and 2–3 stem leaves that are shorter and broader and the golden *R. setifolia* of sandy places with 3–6 leaves.

④ Sparaxis bulbifera
botterblom

  to 45cm   September   October

A geophyte with a globose corm and finely fibrous tunics. The stem bears numerous cormlets after blooming. The leaves are lance-shaped. The white to cream flowers have a pale yellow center, rarely with a blackish spot, are unscented and are 2–5 per spike. It grows on wet sandy or limestone substrates from Darling to Agulhas.

The endangered *Sparaxis grandiflora* is similar to *S. bulbifera* but smaller (10–25 cm), branches below the ground, if at all, and bears only a few cormlets in the lowest joints.

① Watsonia schlechteri

February   November to

to 1m

Plants grow singly, or in small clumps on rocky exposed slopes on Grootbos. Corms are depressed, globose, 30–50 mm in diameter, tunics brown, leaves 3–4, the lower 2–3 more or less basal, and uppermost sheathing the stem, half to two thirds as tall as the plant. The leaves are 6–15 mm wide, the mid-vein and margins heavily thickened. The flowers are bright red-orange, paler in the tube. Flowering is usually stimulated by fire but plants can bloom in mature veld providing the vegetation is not more than 60 cm high. This is a mountain species, found between Ceres and the Kouga Mountains in the southern Cape.

② Watsonia stenosiphon

September   October

to 45cm

This species has a depressed, globose corm, 15–20 mm in diameter with a grey–brown tunic. It has 3–4 leaves, the lower 3 basal, about half as long as the plant, 5–12 mm wide with the mid-vein barely evident and margins not or only slightly thickened. Flowers are uniformly salmon-orange, often with a darker line in the lower midline of the lower three tepals. The species is distinguished by its unusually long narrow perianth tube (stenosiphon = narrow tubed). It blooms most profusely following fires. The pollinators are most likely butterflies in view of the orange colour and slender perianth tube. It is restricted to coarse rocky sandstone soils in flat areas at the foot of coastal ranges between Kleinmond and Cape Infanta.

9. HEMEROCALLIDACEAE

Day lily family

③ Caesia contorta
sokkiesblom, blue grass lily

March   November to

to 30cm

A rhizomatous geophyte with untidy sprawling stems and strap-shaped leaves. It has small nodding blue flowers with rough filaments striped blue and white, the tepals twisting as they fade. It is widespread on flats and slopes between Namaqualand and the Eastern Cape.

10. ASPHODELACEAE

Aloe family

④ Bulbine foleyi

February   October to

to 40cm

A tufted perennial with tuberous rootstock, linear leaves, usually dry at flowering and enclosed at the base with a long fibrous neck. Its yellow, fragrant flowers are in a long dense raceme and it occurs on sandstone slopes between Clanwilliam and Albertinia.

❶ Bulbine lagopus
geelkatstert

July   December

A tufted geophyte with wiry roots and a tuft of narrow, linear, basal leaves. Its yellow flowers, each only lasting one day, are crowded in a dense, elongated raceme on an unbranched flowering stalk. The fruits are globular and carried upright on pedicels, 10–15 mm long. The fresh leaves and roots are used medicinally. The leaf sap is anti-bacterial and anti-fungal and is widely used for the treatment of wounds, burns, rashes, itches, ringworm, cracked lips and herpes. It is widespread in the Western Cape up to Lesotho.

Other species of Bulbine recorded on Grootbos are the annual of coastal sands *B. annua* with crowded cylindrical leaves and crowded flowers and *B. favosa* of sandy and limestone flats, with spaced, scented flowers.

❷ Kniphofia uvaria
red hot poker

March   September to

A rhizomatous perennial, often growing in small clumps in damp areas along streams and on sandstone slopes. It has channelled, fibrous leaves and bears orange to greenish yellow flowers in dense oblong to globular racemes; floral bracts are oval and 3–9 mm long. It is bird pollinated, most profuse following fires and grows from Namaqualand to the Eastern Cape.

❸ Trachyandra ciliata
veldkool

July   September

A sprawling rhizomatous perennial with fleshy swollen roots and soft, spongy, sprawling channelled leaves that are usually hairy. It bears white flowers in an elongated raceme that is unbranched or sparsely branched and usually hairy. The fruits are pendant shaped, hairless and 6–14 mm long. Young flower shoots can be eaten before the flowers open. A coastal species from Namaqualand to the Eastern Cape.

❹ Trachyandra hirsuta

September   December

A tuberous perennial with a fan of stiff hairy flat leaves 7–40 cm long and 5–20 mm wide, and wiry roots. The flowers are white in a sparsely branched raceme. It occurs on lower mountain slopes and flats usually in renosterveld, sometimes in marshes from Piketberg to Cape Agulhas.

❺ Trachyandra revoluta

August   November

A tuberous perennial with swollen roots and many linear, rough textured leaves that are sheathed. It has white, nodding flowers in a divaricate panicle with recurved tepals and the base of the peduncle is scabrid. It grows over a wide area from the Richtersveld to Port Alfred.

10. ASPHODELACEAE

1 Trachyandra sabulosa

September   October

A tuberous perennial with many wiry roots. The many narrow, linear leaves are soft and usually roughly hairy. It has white flowers in a roughly glandular-hairy, trailing, unbranched raceme. Fruits are stalked, 7–9 mm long and densely covered with branched protuberances on long stalks. A species of coastal sandy flats from Hopefield to Cape Agulhas.

Trachyandra tabularis grows in dune strandveld on Groootbos and is sparingly branched with flowers on an ascending raceme, and has 9 mm long fruits.

11. ALLIACEAE

Onion family

2 Tulbaghia alliacea
wild garlic

March   May

A clump-forming, rhizomatous geophyte with linear leaves and brownish to green flowers, the mouth ornamented by a fleshy cylindrical orange corona. The flowers are stalked and borne on a long flower head stalk. The flowers have a sweet honey-coconut scent at night. It occurs throughout southern Africa on clay or gravel soils.

Tulbaghia capensis grows on rocky mountain sandstone and the corona has six lobes.

12. AMARYLLIDACEAE

Amaryllis family

3 Brunsvigia orientalis
candelabra flower

February   April

A spectacular bulbous geophyte that bears a head of many asymmetrical flowers 50–60 mm long. The flowers are followed by the large dry tumbling fruiting heads that detach and roll with the wind, dispersing their seeds as they go. After flowering, about 4 large (15–23 cm long and 7–12 cm wide) tongue-shaped leaves emerge and spread out on the ground. It is pollinated by sunbirds and is common on the coastal plains between Saldanha Bay and Knysna.

Brunsvigia and *Haemanthus* species use their leaves in the winter and spring to store up resources for flowering in the driest times of the year. By February and March when their magnificent flowers appear, the leaves have shrivelled up and disappeared. By flowering in the driest times of the year there is little chance of their pollen getting wet and seeds are released during the wet winter months that follow.

❶ Cyrtanthus leucanthus
witbergpypie

A bulbous geophyte with a hollow flowering stem bearing up to three pale cream, scented flowers that are each 40 mm long. The leaves are approximately two-thirds as long as the stem and only appear once flowering is completed. It is most profuse in the first year following a veld fire and is a local endemic that is restricted to the area between Betty's Bay and Potberg on sandstone or limestone soils.

❷ Haemanthus coccineus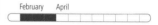
April fool, paintbrush flower

A bulbous geophyte with a speckled and barred flowering stem that is 6–20 cm long. It has a crowded group of red flowers at the apex that are cupped by matching, overlapping spathe bracts. Once flowering is complete, two large, leathery, smooth, tongue shaped leaves appear (up to 20 cm wide), curving out and downwards. The seeds mature and germinate just in time for winter's first rain showers. It occurs in forest scrub and open veld from sea level to the lower mountain slopes from Namaqualand to the Eastern Cape.

❸ Haemanthus sanguineus
veldskoenblaar

Similar to *H. coccineus* but with a rough-textured, unspeckled stem and crowded pink or red flowerheads. The leaves are pressed to the ground and are usually broader than long. A species that flowers mostly after fire and grows on lower slopes from the Nardouw Mountains to Port Elizabeth.

❹ Nerine humilis

A geophyte with 4–6 strap-shaped, dull-green leaves that are dry or green at flowering time. It has 1–8 pale to deep pink flowers in a loose umbel. It grows on loamy and sandstone soils amongst rocks between Clanwilliam and the Baviaanskloof Mountains in the Eastern Cape. On Grootbos there are a few specimens growing amongst the Milkwood trees at the Growing the Future project on Steynsbos.

1 **Agapanthus africanus**
blue lily

April   December to

This well known species has thick tuberous rhizomes, strap-like leaves and a cluster of flowers on a long stalk. The larger, showy *Agapanthus praecox*, erroneously known by this name, is tolerant to a wide range of soil and climatic conditions and is one of the most commonly grown ornamentals in the world. *A. africanus* is restricted to acidic soils and is not suited for cultivation. It flowers mostly after fire, and grows on the upper sandstone slopes on Grootbos. It has a natural distribution from the Cape Peninsula to Swellendam.

14. ASPARAGACEAE

Asparagus family

2 **Asparagus aethiopicus**

January   June

A spiny climber with pale, ribbed stems and hooked spines. It bears stiff, peg-like false leaves in clusters of 4–6 and racemes of fragrant, star-like white flowers. The young shoots are edible and can be eaten like commercial asparagus. It is widespread from Namaqualand to the Eastern Cape.

3 **Asparagus asparagoides**
bridal creeper

July   September

A scrambler with many small, spindle-shaped tubers arising directly from the rhizome. It has oval false leaves and bears solitary nodding white flowers in its axils, the tepals joined below into a short tube and the stamens erect in the centre. It is widespread throughout southern Africa.

4 **Asparagus capensis**
katdoring

April   August

An erect, shiny shrub with spines in threes. The stems look like bottle brushes with whorls of short shoots bearing needle-like false leaves mostly in clusters of five. It bears one or two star-shaped, rose scented white flowers and is widespread on stony slopes from Namibia to the Eastern Cape.

5 **Asparagus rubicundus**
wild asparagus, katdoring

March   August

An erect, spiny shrub with glossy, dark brown stems covered with spreading spines and bearing thread-like false leaves in clusters of about 10. It bears one or two star-shaped white flowers in the axils of the tufts. A plant that has left many a Grootbos visitors with scratches on their legs. It grows in a wide area from Namaqualand to the Eastern Cape.

14. ASPARAGACEAE

① Asparagus scandens

January   September to

A scandent shrub with false leaves in threes, that grow in one plane with a solitary smaller one opposing a larger pair. There are one to three flowers in the axils of the false leaves. It grows in forests from the Gifberg to the Tsitsikamma.

② Asparagus volubilis

June   October

A scandent shrub with false leaves with several leaves that are narrow and elliptic in shape. The flowers are nodding and solitary in the axils of the false leaves. It is a common species in coastal scrub and forest from Citrusdal to the Eastern Cape.

Two other Asparagus species have been recorded on Grootbos, the scrambling *A. ovatus* in dune strandveld with glossy, oval false leaves and nodding white flowers with brown midribs and the erect shrub *Asparagus stipulaceus* with minutely ribbed stems and spines in threes on sandstone fynbos.

15. HYACINTHACEAE

③ Albuca fragrans

September   October

A bulbous perennial with 2–4 narrow, channelled leaves clasping the stem at the base. It bears racemes that droop in bud, with nodding yellow flowers with broad green bands, 15–25 mm long; the outer anthers are slightly smaller. A predominantly coastal species that grows from the Bokkeveld Mountains to Gansbaai.

④ Albuca juncifolia

September   October

A bulbous perennial with 4–10 slender, stiff leaves that are channelled below, but often cylindrical above. The leaves do not clasp the stem below. It bears racemes that droop at the tips, with fragrant, nodding yellow flowers that have broad green bands, 15–25 mm long. The inner petals have a hinged flap at the tip and the outer stamens are sterile. It grows from the West Coast to the southern Cape.

⑤ Albuca flaccida

August   October

A bulbous perennial with membranous bulb tunics and 3–5 channelled, fleshy leaves that clasp the stem near its base. It has nodding, slightly fragrant flowers that are mostly yellow, sometimes with green keels (15–25 mm long). The inner tepals are hinged above and the outer stamens are sterile. It grows in coastal sands from southern Namaqualand to Stilbaai.

Other species on Grootbos are *Albuca acuminata*, which grows to 30 cm and has bulb scales that are fibrous above and several channelled leaves that are clasping above, *A. cooperi* that has leaves that are warty below and *Albuca maxima* that grows to 1.5 m, and has 4–6 fleshy lance-shaped leaves and nodding white flowers with broad green bands.

❶ Drimia exuviata

September   October

A bulbous perennial with a few erect, quill-like, leathery leaves, 3–4 mm in diameter. The leaves are wrapped below in a horizontally barred sheath. It bears star-shaped, rose-scented, white flowers that are often flushed with purple and have dark keels. It is widespread from Namaqualand to the Eastern Cape.

❷ Drimia media

January   March

A bulbous perennial with 10–20 erect, semi-terete leaves (30 x 0.3 cm) present at flowering. Flowers are silvery purple-brown and occur in a lax cylindrical raceme. The species is found on sandy coastal flats and slopes from Saldanha to Knysna

The smaller *Drimia filifolia*, characterised by leaves approximately 1 mm in diameter, has also been recorded on sandstone slopes on Grootbos

❸ Lachenalia bulbifera
rooi viooltjie

April   September

A bulbous plant with one or two strap-shaped leaves, which may be heavily spotted or unspotted on their upper surfaces. The flowerhead consists of hanging, tubular flowers which are orange-red with dark green to purple tips, the inner tepals only slightly longer than the outer, the anthers concealed within the flowers. It grows on sandy soils, dunes and rocky outcrops from the West Coast to Mossel Bay.

① Lachenalia lutzeyeri

October   November

One of the endemics to Grootbos, this species was first collected by Heiner Lutzeyer on the upper slopes of Witkransberg after a small fire in November 2004. It was sent to Kirstenbosch and thought to be an unusual form of *Lachenalia montana* that also grows in the area. However, subsequent to the huge, February 2006 fire thousands of this 'unusual form' of *L. montana* appeared on the sandstone ridges of the reserve and it was subsequently classified as a new species, endemic to Grootbos, *Lachenalia lutzeyeri*. Remarkably, although many leaves were seen in the second year following the fire, only three plants were seen flowering and by year three it had all but disappeared from the landscape – waiting underground for the next fire to bloom and seed!

This species has an unusually deep-seated, globose, (20–25 mm), white bulb with membranous, dark brown outer tunics and many roots. The one or two leaves are narrowly lance-shaped (85–290 × 4–13 mm), prostrate, spreading or suberect and yellowish green or pale to deep maroon. The leaf surface is plain or with large dark green, brown or maroon flattened pustules and the margins are thickened. The leaf clasps the stem underground with about 85 mm underground and only a short portion of 15 mm above ground. The many flowers are in a moderately dense raceme 50–120 mm long, with a sterile apex up to 10 mm long. The flower stalk is green and unmarked, or yellowish green and heavily marked with minute maroon speckles or small to large maroon blotches. The flowers are oblong, nodding and yellowish cream with dark green or brown gibbosities, with a moderately strong, soapy-sweet scent, fading to dull maroon and ascending in fruit. The perianth tube is cup-shaped, pale yellowish cream and 2–3 mm long.

Lachenalia lutzeyeri is presently only known from the type locality on Witkransberg on Grootbos. It has remained undetected until recently owing to its extremely erratic flowering, due to its dependence on summer or early autumn fires, coupled with its very late flowering period and the slim chance of it being recognised as a distinct taxon due to its superficial similarity to other members of the genus. *L. lutzeyeri* is remarkable in being one of only three members of this genus known to be entirely dependent on the effects of fire for flowering to occur. The others being *L. montana* and *L. sargeantii*.

The species grows in full sun in open aspects or between Table Mountain Sandstone boulders, on a number of ridges on the reserve between about 350 and 400 m above sea level.

'*Lachenalia lutzeyeri* is named in honour of Heiner Lutzeyer of Grootbos Private Nature Reserve near Gansbaai, who discovered this species and made the first collection of plants, in recognition of the wonderful contribution that he has made to nature conservation in this part of the southern Cape.'

(Duncan and Edwards 2007)

❶ Lachenalia rosea

August   December

A bulbous plant with one or two lance-shaped leaves that are plain or blotched with maroon or brown markings. The flowers are narrowly bell-shaped and pink or a combination of blue and pink. It grows mainly in coastal sands from the Cape Peninsula to Knysna.

❷ Lachenalia rubida
sandklossie

March   July

A geophyte with one or two lance- or strap-shaped leaves plain green or spotted with darker green or purple. The flowers are on a short stalk, nodding and cylindrical in shape. They are plain or densely spotted with pink or red, the perianth 20–32 mm long and anthers included. It is a species of sandy coastal flats and has a natural distribution from Hondeklip Bay to the Cape Peninsula and eastwards to George.

❸ Lachenalia variegata

  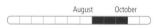

August   October

A bulbous geophyte with a single, lance- or strap-shaped leaf with thickened, undulating margins. The narrow, bell-shaped flowers are greenish grey with darker green, blue, purple, or brown markings and white tips. It grows mainly in deep coastal sands from Clanwilliam to the Cape Peninsula.

❹ Massonia pustulata
hedgehog lily

May   July

A low, ground-hugging, bulbous plant with two broad, flat, leathery leaves approximately 15 cm long. The leaves are characterised by rough, blistered (pustulate) upper surfaces. The flowers are densely clustered between the two leaves and are creamy-white, pink or yellow. This species is pollinated by honeybees and butterflies in search of the nectar held in the bottom of the elongate floral tubes. It is a widespread species, common on coastal sands and limestone on Grootbos, and has a natural distribution from Namaqualand to Port Elizabeth and the Karoo.

15. HYACINTHACEAE

1 Ornithogalum thyrsoides
chinkerinchee

A bulbous species with about seven slender, linear to lance-shaped, channelled leaves that are sometimes dry at flowering. The flowers are white with dark, grey-green centres that are clustered at the top of the flowering stem. The plants are toxic to livestock and the flowers were once extensively exported to Europe for the Christmas flower trade. It grows on sandy flats and lower slopes, often in wet areas from Namaqualand to just south of Grootbos at Pearly Beach.

O. juncifolium with sub-erect, strongly ribbed leaves and small white flowers that open only a few at a time, also grows on Grootbos.

16. HAEMODORACEAE

Bloodroot family

2 Wachendorfia paniculata
rooikanol, spinnekopblom

A slender, hairy perennial with reddish tuberous roots and a fan of pleated leaves that are up to 40 cm long. The yellow flowers are up to 25 mm long and usually have dark markings. The bracts are papery and one of the three stamens grows in a direction opposite from the off-centre style, reducing the chance of self-pollination. The species is pollinated by bees and horseflies and uses three orange dots to help guide insects to its hidden nectar. It flowers abundantly after fire and grows in well-drained soils from Clanwilliam to Port Elizabeth.

The much taller *W. thyrsiflora* reaches 1 m and is found in marshes and wet areas on the reserve.

17. CYPERACEAE

Sedge family

3 Cyperus thunbergii

A robust, tufted perennial with a stiff 3-sided solid stem and basal leaves slightly shorter than the stem. The stalks of the flower spikes are of unequal length and the flower clusters are surrounded by a number of bristly, leafy bracts. This species occurs in damp places on Grootbos and is widespread in coastal regions from Clanwilliam to KwaZulu-Natal.

4 Hellmuthia membranacea
biesie

A tufted, reed-like perennial with a few small (10–50 mm long) leaves at the base of the flower stalk. It has dark brown, clustered spikelets at the tip of the leafless stems. It is found on coastal sands from Saldanha Bay to Knysna.

Cape reeds, biesies and dekriet are some of the common names that have been applied to members of the South African family of Restionaceae. There are some 480 species of Restionaceae globally, of which 330 are found in the Cape Floristic Region, while Grootbos is home to 21 different species in this family. They are the unique distinguishing family of the fynbos. Simply put, if you can't see restios then you are not in fynbos! The distribution range over all the southern continents has led to suggestions that the family is ancient, dating to as far back as 60 million years ago, when the southern continents were still in close proximity to each other, forming the supercontinent Gondwana.

① Elegia tectorum   to 1m
dekriet

A tufted perennial with leaf sheaths that drop off. The flowers are less than 3 mm long with petals that are smooth, or hairy, only in the upper half. Well known by its previous name *Chondropetalum tectorum* as a horticultural species that grows well in a variety of soils and climatic conditions. This species is found on wet sandstone flats on Grootbos and has a natural distribution stretching from Clanwilliam to Port Elizabeth.

While *Thamnochortus insignis* and *T. erectus* are favoured by the thatching industry, *Elegia tectorum* is also sometimes used for thatch. The taller growing version from the West Coast is favoured for thatch harvesting, while the shorter version from our area is used mainly for wild flower bouquets.

② Elegia juncea   to 80cm

A tufted perennial with male and female flowers on separate plants. The stem sheaths are deciduous and the plant has spreading rhizomes. It grows on the upper sandstone slopes on Grootbos, and has a natural distribution from the Grootwinterhoek Mountains to the Cape Peninsula and eastwards to the Swartberg Mountains.

③ Elegia thyrsifera   to 1.4m

This beautiful restio forms dense stands on the middle north- and west-facing slopes of the reserve. It has stem sheaths that are deciduous and large spathellae with bracts shorter than the flowers. It grows on mountain slopes from the Cape Peninsula to Knysna and has great potential as a garden restio for coastal gardens.

Other Elegia species on Grootbos are *E. filacea* with slender culms to 50 cm in mountain fynbos and *Elegia muirii* with persistent sheaths in limestone fynbos.

❶ Ischyrolepis leptoclados

June July

besemriet, broom reed

A spreading (rhizomatous) plant with branched stems and single spikelets (flowers) at the end of the stems. The plants tend to grow on cool, moist slopes on Grootbos and are taller and more finely branched than the similar *I. eleocharis*, which is common on the open sandy flats of the Reserve. This species is harvested for wild flower bouquets as well as for brooms! It grows naturally on coastal dunes and limestone outcrops from Betty's Bay to Knysna.

The tangled, fountain-shaped *Ischyrolepis capensis* only reaches 50 cm and has branched, warty stems.

❷ Restio triticeus

February April

A fountain-shaped reed with stems that have flat-topped, whitish tubercles (warts). The culms often have sterile branches below. It is widespread on sandstone soils of lower slopes from Malmesbury to the Eastern Cape.

Restio tetragonus has four-sided square stems and prefers seeps and stream banks in the reserve.

❸ Thamnochortus erectus

September October

wyfieriet, somersriet

The tallest restio on Grootbos, growing as a large, fountain-shaped tussock. It has unbranched stems. In female spikelets the bracts are erect and designed to catch pollen. The male spikelets hang loosely, blowing in the wind, releasing pollen in the spring. The female culms are generally somewhat thicker than the males and both are able to resprout from underground culms after fire or harvesting. It is harvested in the summer and is commonly known as 'somersriet' or 'wyfieriet'. Although fast growing (it can reach harvestable lengths within a year) and widely distributed, it is not as popular in the thatching trade as *T. insignis* (the Albertinia thatching reed – or mannetjiesriet), since wyfiesriet is thinner, not as tall and likely to break at the nodes, making a less durable thatch. Harvesting of this species should only take place following seed set from November to February. This species is not at present threatened by harvesting. It grows over a large distribution on dune sands from Malmesbury through the Agulhas Plain to Knysna.

❹ Thamnochortus fraternus

April May

A fountain-shaped reed with erect, narrow, pointed bracts on the stems. The male and female flowers are on separate plants and the female spikelets are about 20 mm long. It occurs on coastal limestone outcrops from False Bay to the Agulhas area and is threatened by coastal development and invasive alien plants.

18. RESTIONACEAE

Thamnochortus lucens grows to 60 cm, is found in mountain fynbos on the reserve and has many branched, sterile culms.

❶ Willdenowia teres

September

A restio with smooth, branched stems and persistent sheaths that loosely wrap around the stem. The species is easy to identify on the basis of its characteristic black nuts with their green elaiosomes. These are used to attract ants for ant dispersal underground. The species is common in the dune strandveld on the reserve and has a natural distribution from the Kamiesberg to Uitenhage

All restios are wind pollinated, leading to fascinating adaptations of the flowers to release and catch pollen. They are also all dioecious (two homes) and the male and female flowers are borne on separate plants. This is primarily so that plants can't fertilise themselves and has resulted in structurally different male and female plants.

19. RANUNCULACEAE

❷ Anemone anemonoides

January   September to

(=*Knowltonia anemonoides*) A thinly silky, tufted perennial with leathery leaves that are divided twice or three times into evenly toothed, oval-shaped segments that are hairy below. It bears clusters of greenish-white to purple flowers on flower stalks that are usually much longer than the leaves. The fruits are hairy. It grows on rocky slopes from Tulbagh to the Cape Peninsula and eastwards to Riversdale, and flowers mostly after fire.

❸ Anemone vesicatoria
katjiedrieblaar, tooth ache leaf

August   October

(=*Knowltonia vesicatoria*) A hairless, tufted perennial with a short rhizome and fleshy roots that has once- or twice-divided leathery leaves with toothed margins. It bears clusters of white to yellowish-green flowers on flower stalks that are about as long as the leaves. The plant is an old Cape remedy for back pain and rheumatism. Decoctions of the roots, mixed with *Pelargonium* roots, have been used to treat colds and influenza. The fresh roots and leaves are sniffed for headaches or may be applied to gums or teeth to alleviate toothache. It is common in or around the Milkwood forests on Grootbos.

The Proteaeceae are a family of some 330 species of varying colour, form and shape. The name is said to come from Proteus, Neptune's herdsman, who could avoid evildoers by changing himself into any shape he desired. The plants that bear his name are well represented on Grootbos with 15 species ranging from the low, ground creeping *Leucospermum prostratum* to the magnificent *Protea cynaroides*. All except two of these grow along the Protea trail that traverses Swartkransberg.

❶ Aulax umbellata
broad-leaf featherbush

  to 2.5m

February | November to

An erect shrub with a single main stem and linear to oblanceolate leaves. The male and female flowers are borne on separate plants, with the male being a lax raceme of 4–10 at the end of the flowering branches. The female flowerhead is a globose cup formed by 8–15 inwardly curved bundles of axillary branches, covered externally with leaf-like bracts and bearing stalked female flowers inside on a central column. This species is highly social, often found in large colonies and is common on Grootbos on the plateau between Witkransberg and Swartkransberg. It grows on coastal lowlands from the Kogelberg to the Riversdale Flats.

❷ Leucadendron salignum
common sunshine conebush, geelbos

 to 2m

April | November

A multi-stemmed shrub with a persistent rootstock enabling it to resprout after fires. It is usually seen as a sprawling shrub less than 1m tall, but can grow taller. The leaves are hairless and the involucral leaves (leaves around the flowers) are ivory to yellow coloured. The male and females are separate plants with the female cones being round (*ca.* 20 mm wide) and retained on the plants for several years. The male flowerhead is 10–16 mm long and 9–12 mm across, egg-shaped and has a sweet, yeasty smell. This is the most widespread member of the Protea family in the fynbos, occurring from the Bokkeveld Escarpment to the Cape Peninsula and through to the Eastern Cape. It occurs on a wide range of soil types, from sea level to an altitude of 2 000 m and is quite variable in leaf size as well as leaf- and bract colour. On Grootbos it is a good indicator of acid soils and the Overberg sandstone fynbos vegetation type.

Leucadredon salignum is characterised by a wide variation of leaves and bracts, from greenish-yellow to vivid orange-red and the species adapts well to rigorous pruning. As a result, the species makes an excellent candidate for the wild flower industry and cultivar breeding. There are a range of plants in cultivation, which differ markedly from the usual parent species, most often in growth form, leaf- and bract colour and flowering time. They may be either selections, known as 'cultivars' or hybrids which are 'crosses' between *L. salignum* and other species. A well known example is *L. x* 'Safari Sunset', a hybrid of *L. laureolum x L. salignum*. This is one of the best known leucadendron's and an export flower crop in several countries.

L. xanthoconus is also found on the sandstone slope on Grootbos but has a single stem from the base and often slightly more silvery-green leaves.

① Leucadendron coniferum

August   September

dune conebush

This large bush or small tree has a stout trunk and narrow leaves with sharp tips that are hairless when mature. Male and females are separate bushes. The female cones are about 40 mm long and 30 mm in diameter and are held on the bush for a number of years. This phenomenon, known as serotiny, ensures that the seeds are protected within the canopy of the plant until fire, when the mother bush is killed and the cones open within a few days to be released into the nutrient-rich, post-fire soils. Not only have vital, limited nutrients been returned to the soils but the post-fire environment is free of rodents and conditions are ideal for germination. This species was once widespread on the Cape Flats where its habitat has been lost to urban sprawl. It is now found only on the Cape Peninsula and from Kogelberg to the Soetanysberg on the Agulhas Plain where it grows between 0–300 m on wind-blown sands.

② Leucadendron spissifolium

August   October

common spear-leaf conebush

A shrub with a persistent rootstock enabling it to resprout after fire. The hairless, shiny red-tipped leaves are slightly twisted along the axis. The male cones are up to 18 mm and the female 15 mm in diameter, with a faint lemon scent, and are haloed by ivory-coloured pointed involucral leaves (leaves around the cone). Female flowers emerge up the flanks of the cone, and the cones are retained until the parent plants are killed by fire. Interestingly, the leaves are larger in females than in the males. This is a common feature of leucadendrons as the female requires stronger stems and larger leaves to feed and support its canopy stored seed bank until the seeds are released after fires. Typical of resprouting plants, this species is not found in dense stands, but rather scattered across the landscape. It has a wide distribution growing on damp south-facing sandstone slopes from the Gifberg to the Cape Peninsula, Kogelberg, Agulhas Plain and the Langeberg.

③ Leucadendron tinctum

July

spicy conebush, toffee-apple

A bushy, spreading shrub with a single main stem. It has hairy branches and oblong to lance-shaped blue-green leaves that are hairless and orientated downward at the base and curving upward at the tip. The leaves become larger and more crowded towards the tips of the branches, forming an opulent, loose yellow, reddening cup of involucral leaves around the flower heads, the colour intensifying at flowering time. The spice-scented flowers are constricted by an

encircling collar of oily, yellow, tightly recurved involucral bracts (that taste terrible and must be acting to protect the flowers from insects), emerging as a cluster on the summit of the cone. The fruits are nut-like, thought to be rodent dispersed and are held in yellow, reddening cones (the toffee-apples!) until they are released in late summer. This species is found on stony, acidic soils from Kleinmond through to the Langeberg Mountains.

① Leucospermum patersonii

August   November

silver-edge pincushion

A single-stemmed shrub to small tree with oblong leaves that have 3–8 glandular teeth on their tips. The flowerheads are orange turning crimson as they mature. The pollen presenter is large and hoof shaped. Fruits are released two months after flowering. A popular species for the wild flower industry on the Agulhus Plain. This species is restricted to limestone between Kleinmond and the Elim Flats near Cape Agulhas. It has become locally extinct around Hermanus and some of the best remaining stands of this beautiful pincushion are found on the limestone hills of Grootbos.

The bright orange flowers of *Leucospermum pattersonii* act as a 'landing pad' for sugarbirds which delve down into the flower to extract nectar. The pollen is placed onto their heads by the long incurved styles. The plant only produces a few large, precious seeds per flower head. These ripen by late summer and drop to the ground where their waxy elaisome (seed cover) attracts indigenous ants who carry the seed underground into their nests (see inset). Once in the nests, the ants devour the energy rich seed coating, leaving the seed safely 'planted' out of harms way. Ants are responsible for dispersing approximately 170 species of Proteaceae and many other species in the Cape flora. The seeds lay dormant underground until nutrients from fire leach down through the earth. These nutrients, together with sufficient moisture and cool winter temperatures break the dormancy, causing the seeds to germinate in the first winter following fire. Without the sugarbirds, the ants, the fire and our cool Cape winters, this species would be unable to reproduce and play its keystone role in the ecology of fynbos.

① Leucospermum prostratum
yellow trailing pincushion

to 30cm — July December

A trailing perennial, up to 4 m across with numerous slender unbranched stems arising from an underground rootstock (resprouts after fire). The vertical, olive-green leaves are covered with hairs, (up to 40 mm long by 2–6 mm wide), with no glandular teeth. It has clusters of up to three spherical, sweetly-scented flowerheads, 20–25 mm in diameter, which open bright yellow and turn orange with age (see inset). It occurs on sandstones from Kogelberg to the Elim Flats. The flowers of this species release a sweet, yeasty scent and are pollinated by rodents.

② Mimetes cucullatus
common pagoda, rooistompie

to 2m — All year

A shrub with many erect stems arising from a large underground rootstock, enabling the plant to survive and resprout after fires. It has oblong to elliptic, hairless leaves that are between 25–55 mm long and 5–20 mm wide. The flowerhead is cylindrical, 60–100 mm long and topped by flat, red reduced leaves. Each headlet (group of flowers) is made up of 4–7 flowers that are subtended and clasped from above by an orange-red, cowl-shaped leaf. These leaves act to attract bird pollinators to the flower. The fruits are oval shaped to cylindrical and have a prominent elaiosome at either end, which is used to attract ants for dispersal safely underground. The species is widespread in the fynbos on sandstone slopes between 0–1 200 m. It occurs from the Bokkeveld to Cape Agulhas and eastwards to the Kouga Mountains.

The protea flower is not a flower, but a flower head or inflorescence, made up of many individual flowers grouped together on a rounded base or receptacle. What looks like the 'petals' of the protea 'flower' are modified leaves known as floral or involucral bracts. Inside the cup of involucral bracts are many long, narrow flowers massed together in the centre.

③ Protea acaulos
common ground sugarbush

to 15cm — June November

A low, creeping shrub to 1 m across, with underground branches and a rootstock. It has trailing, hairless stems and variable, hairless, leathery leaves with a base tapering gradually or abruptly to a stalk. The leaves point vertically from a horizontal stem and are linear to broadly oval-shaped, 60–250 mm long, 6–70 mm wide. The flowerheads are cup-shaped, 30–60 mm across, with green, hairless flowering bracts with red tips. This species is pollinated by rodents and grows in sandy soils from 0–1 500 m from the Cape Peninsula to the Cederberg and eastwards to the Riviersonderend Mountains.

① Protea cynaroides
king protea

All year

A woody, resprouting shrub with thick stems and large dark green, glossy leaves. Most plants on Grootbos are about one metre in height when mature, but may vary according to locality across their distribution range and habitat from 35 cm to 2 m in height. The 'flowers' of *Protea cynaroides* are actually flower heads with a collection of flowers in the centre, surrounded by large colourful bracts. The flowerheads vary in size, from about 120 mm to 300 mm in diameter. The colour of the bracts varies from a creamy white (typical on Grootbos) to a deep crimson red.

The flower bud of *Protea cynaroides* looks remarkably like the globe artichoke vegetable with the Latin name of *Cynara scolymus*, which led the botanist Linnaeus to give it the species name *cynaroides*. *Protea cynaroides* has one of the widest distribution ranges of all the Proteaceae and occurs from the Cedarberg to Grahamstown on all mountain ranges in this area, except for the dry interior ranges, and at all elevations, from sea level to 1 500 m.

This species is South Africa's national flower and prized worldwide as a magnificent cut flower. The combination of the different climatic conditions with the large range of localities has resulted in a large variety of leaf- and flower sizes, as well as flower colours and flowering times. The different forms retain these characteristics even when grown under the same conditions on a commercial scale. This has made it possible to grow *Protea cynaroides* as a cut flower for a wide variety of export markets, where the flowers are needed at different times of the year.

② Protea obtusifolia
bredasdorp protea, limestone sugarbush

April   September

A single-stemmed, erect shrub with upward curving, leathery, rich dark green leaves that are broadly lance-shaped, 100–150 x 20–40 mm, with the broadest part above the middle (oblanceolate), an obtuse to rounded apex, and tapering to a distinct petiole. It has red and occasionally cream flowerheads. The pointed, cone-shaped seedheads retain seeds for many years until they are released after fire. This species is endemic to limestone fynbos in the area and on Grootbos is a strong indicator of limestone soils. While this species is naturally only found on limestone, it thrives in alkaline or acidic soils, making it one of the most adaptable proteas for gardens. Populations used to occur as far west as Hermanus and Onrust but they have been wiped out by urban development. It now occurs naturally from Gansbaai to the Riversdale Flats and is a favoured food source for Cape sugarbirds.

Protea obtusifolia is pollinated by the Cape sugarbird *Promerops cafer*, one of six birds endemic to the Cape flora. This bird is easily recognisable by a spot of yellow under its tail and the very long tail feathers present in males. The male's tail is 34–44 cm long, and the shorter-tailed, shorter-billed, and paler breasted female 25–29 cm long. This remarkable

bird's main flight feathers are arranged in such a way that when the bird beats its wings, a frrt-frrt sound is made with the intention of attracting females. It is a specialist nectar feeder, using its long, sharp beak and brush-tipped tongue to reach the nectar of a variety of Proteaceae. The Sugarbird pushes its head between the masses of flowers and so doing rubs pollen onto its head. It then flies off to another bush and transfers its load of pollen to other flowers. It visits about 300 flower-heads a day during autumn and winter to satisfy its energy requirements. While the sugarbird's staple diet is nectar, it will also eat spiders and insects. It has sharp claws to enable it to cling onto flowers for feeding even in strong winds.

① Protea longifolia
long-leaf sugarbush

An almost erect to sprawling shrub with a single main trunk and stems that are hairless when mature. It has upward curving leaves, 90–200 mm long, 5–17 mm wide, tapering at the base. The greenish, pink or white flowerheads are oblong-shaped with a central, pointed, black woolly cone. *P.longifolia* is able to cross with many other Protea species. It grows on acidic soils from Du Toitskloof to Riviersonderend and the Bredasdorp Mountains and Elim Flats. On Grootbos it is most common on ironstone or ferricrete soils.

② Protea repens
common sugarbush

An erect shrub, with a single stem and upright leaves (50–100 mm long, 80 mm wide) with pointed, sticky, cream to pinkish-red bracts, forming cone-shaped seedheads that remain on the plant for several years. It is killed by fire and releases seeds after fire. The copious nectar produced by the flowers is loved by baboons, and was widely used for sugar and syrup (bossiestroop) production by early settlers. It is an excellent addition to any indigenous fynbos garden as the plants are tolerant to a large variation in growing conditions and the flowers produce large amounts of nectar attracting birds, bees and other insects. It is widespread across the entire fynbos region from the Bokkeveld escarpment to Cape Peninsula to Grahamstown.

③ Protea speciosa
brown-beard sugarbush

A sturdy, erect shrub growing from a fire-resistant rootstock. It has leaves with thickened margins that are 90–160 mm long and 10–60 mm wide. The flowerheads have closely packed pink to brown, fringed involucral bracts. Typical of resprouting proteas it occurs as scattered plants and is restricted to acid soils from the Cape Peninsula to Bredasdorp.

① Cotyledon orbiculata
plakkie, pigs ear

All year

A shrubby plant with woody branches and succulent leaves. The large, oval ear-like leaves (100 mm long) are green to light grey, have red margins and a waxy layer on the surface. The stalked, hanging tubular flowers have backward-curled petals and are dusky pink-rose to scarlet. It is common on dunes along the coast and grows in coastal and arid areas in Namibia and South Africa.

The plant is widely used for medicinal purposes. The fleshy part of the leaf is applied to corns and warts to soften and remove them. The warmed leaf juice is used as drops for earache and toothache. This species is common on the coastline at De Kelders and on Danger Point and has been found growing on rocky hillsides on Grootbos.

② Crassula capensis
cape snowdrop

May   November

Small tuberous geophyte that has pairs of delicate, disproportionately large round leaves with a scalloped edge. It has clusters of white (occasionally pink) flowers with 3–8 mm long petals on raised stalks. It typically grows in cool, damp places amongst rocks from Clanwilliam to Riversdale.

③ Crassula dichotoma

September   October

A wiry-stemmed annual that has fleshy, lance-shaped leaves that are obscurely toothed. It bears flat-topped clusters of yellow to orange flowers, often marked with red in the throat. The species is pollinated by melittid bees and some pollen wasps. The petals are 8–15 mm long. It grows on sandy flats from Namibia to Agulhas.

④ Crassula expansa
subsp. filicaulis

All year

A prostrate, succulent shrub with stilt-like roots along the branches and fleshy leaves that are often red. It has small, white, pink or yellow flowers that occur singly along the stems. The plants occur on coastal dunes and flats as well as in sandy pockets in limestone. The species grows from the Cape Peninsula to Port Alfred as well as up the West coast to Namibia.

Crassula expansa subsp. expansa is also found on Grootbos but differs by having green leaves and growing in seasonally inundated wetlands.

❶ Crassula fascicularis
klipblom

September   November

A succulent perennial with stems that bear pointed, slightly fleshy, narrow to lance-shaped leaves that are often hairy-edged. The flowers are jasmine-like and have petals up to 32 mm long. They are white to pale cream or yellow-green and are sometimes pink-tinged. They are fragrant at night and pollinated by Mountain pride butterflies, *Meneris tulbaghia*. These butterflies play an important role in the ecology of the mountainous areas on Grootbos, pollinating a number of plants with large red flowers. *Crassula fascicularis* grows on the upper sandstone slopes of Grootbos and has a natural distribution on sandstone slopes from the Gifberg to Langeberg Mountains.

❷ Crassula subulata

September   October

A shrublet with opposite leaves that are linear-lance-shaped and mostly round in section with stout hairs on margins. The flowers are in rounded, head-like clusters that are about 4 mm long, tubular and cream-coloured. It is found on dry, rocky slopes from the Bokkeveld Mountains to Port Alfred.

A further four Crassula species have been recorded on Grootbos. *Crassula campestris* is a small annual with opposite, imbricate, ovate-triangular leaves growing on sandstone substrate, *C. depressa* is also an annual with obovate leaves restricted to dune and limestone soils, *C. glomerata* is a stiffly erect annual that grows to 15 cm with sessile flowers growing on coastal sands and limestones and *C. natans* is a floating annual in moist depressions or pools.

22. ZYGOPHYLLACEAE

Twinleaf family

❸ Roepera flexuosa
maerbos

June   October

A sprawling shrublet with sessile leaves that are divided into two succulent oval leaflets. It bears golden-yellow flowers with reddish markings that have five petals that are flexed back. The fruits are approximately globular and wider than long with five sutures. It is a coastal species that grows between Veldrif and Knysna.

Other Roepera species on Grootbos are the rare *R. fuscata*, which is very similar to *R. flexuosa* but differs by being erect to 1 m and having 5-angled fruits with ribs, and *R. sessilifolia* with whitish flowers.

The Fabaceae (pea and bean or pod-bearing family) is the second largest flowering plant family after Asteraceae. It contains more than 600 genera and 12 000 species and is found throughout the world. In southern Africa this family is represented by 134 genera and more than 1 300 species and on Grootbos we have recorded 13 genera and 39 species. Ecologically, legumes are well known for fixing nitrogen in the soil through a symbiotic relationship with bacteria. The bacteria infect the roots, forming small growths or nodules. Inside the nodules, atmospheric nitrogen, which the plants cannot utilise, is converted to ammonia, which plants can absorb. The plant supplies sugars for the bacteria, while the bacteria provide the biologically useful nitrogen that the plant absorbs. Many Fabaceae are relatively short lived, proliferating after fire and providing a crucial service of nitrogen-fixing and soil improvement to other slower growing fynbos species that ultimately dominate the landscape.

❶ Aspalathus caledonensis

to 1.2m — August — November

An erect, rod-like shrub that often stands out above surrounding low mountain fynbos. It has flat silvery leaves with the central leaflet (5 mm long, 2 mm wide) about twice the length of the two side leaflets. It has lemon-yellow flowers arranged in a spike-like fashion along much of the plant's length. This species is found on sandy or gravelly slopes of the mountains from Houwhoek to Potberg.

❷ Aspalathus callosa

to 60cm — January — October to

An erect shrublet with 3-foliolate leaves and flat, non-fleshy linear leaflets. It has yellow hair-less flowers, crowded at the tips of its branches. It grows in lowland fynbos between the Cape Peninsula and Bredasdorp.

❸ Aspalathus ciliaris

to 1.5m — February — September to

An erect or sprawling shrub with 3-foliolate leaves, the leaflets are linear and hairless or softly haired. The bright yellow flowers are in terminal heads and fade to red, brown or black. A widespread species that grows on lowland fynbos from Clanwilliam to Humansdorp.

❹ Aspalathus forbesii

to 2.5m — April — July

A shrub with 3-foliolate leaves and almost cylindrical leaflets, 2–8 mm long. It bears white or cream flowers, sometimes with pink on the wings, in terminal heads. The flower-keel is hairless and silky and the upper lobes are deeply separated. This species grows on limestone sands between the Cape Peninsula and Stilbaai.

1 Aspalathus globulosa

October December

A shrublet with needle-like hairy leaflets. The branches end in compact heads of bluish-violet flowers surrounded by white-hairy round leaves. It is found in coastal fynbos from the Cape Peninsula to just past Grootbos near Pearly Beach.

2 Aspalathus sericea

September November

A slender shrublet with rod-like branches and 3-foliolate leaves, the middle leaflet elliptic to lance-shaped, thinly silky. The side leaflets are smaller or completely lacking. The flowers are crowded in terminal spikes, pale yellow and fading brownish. The keel and calyx is softly hairy, wing blades 9–10 mm long. It grows on coastal flats below 300 m from Hopefield to Agulhas.

3 Bolusafra bituminosa
sticky tar-pea

January August to

A sprawling, twining or climbing, resinous-hairy and tar-scented climber that is woody at the base. The leaves have three leaflets and the yellow flowers are borne at the end of long flowering stalks. They give rise to cylindrical pods containing 4–6 seeds. This species is common on mountainsides in mountain fynbos and along streams from Tulbagh to Caledon.

4 Dipogon lignosus
cape sweet pea, klimop

All year

A woody climber with 3-foliolate leaves and diamond shaped leaflets that are greyish beneath. It bears racemes of magenta or pink flowers that are 10–15 mm long. The flowers develop into sickle-shaped 4–6 seeded pods. It is most common in forest margins and grows from Saldanha Bay to the Eastern Cape.

5 Indigofera brachystachya

September November to

A dense, mass-flowering shrub with grey, densely-haired stems and sessile, 5–7 foliolate leaves and narrowly wedge-shaped leaflets that are short-haired above and densely grey-haired beneath. The leaf margins are strongly rolled under. It bears sessile, mauve to pink flowers in dense racemes, with persistant petals and the back of the standard petal has silky white hairs. This species turns the lower dune strandveld on Grootbos pink in July and August each year. It grows on coastal fynbos and limestone from the Cape Peninsula to Agulhas.

① Indigofera incana

July · November

A prostrate, spreading to erect shrublet with 3-foliolate leaves, the leaflets being obovate to oblong in shape and coarsely long hairy. It bears rose to pink flowers in racemes on robust peduncles and occurs in renosterbos-fynbos scrub on lower to middle slopes from Piketberg to Barrydale.

② Indigofera nigromontana

March · June to

An erect spiny shrub with 3-foliolate leaves, the leaflets small, obovate, concave and thinly hairy above. It bears pinkish purple flowers in racemes and grows in karroid shrub, renosterveld and fynbos from Namaqualand to the Great Karoo and Lesotho.

Also on Grootbos *Indigofera angustifolia* is a diffuse, sprawling shrublet with linear leaflets that have a sunken midrib above and pink or red flowers, *I. capillaris* grows on sandstome fynbos, has reddish-brown stems that are often brittle and dark pink, purple, copper or magenta flowers in racemes on slender peduncles more than twice as long as the leaves, and the procumbent *I. porrecta* with furrowed stems and orange-pink to reddish purple flowers in racemes on robust flowering stems.

③ Lessertia frutescens
sutherlandia, kankerbos

July · December

(=*Sutherlandia frutescens*) A shrublet with leaves divided into greyish-green leaflets. This is a much-respected and long-used medicinal plant that is also an attractive garden plant. It has been cultivated in gardens for many years for its fine form, striking color and luminous red-orange flowers that appear in spring. It has bitter, aromatic leaves and is currently being investigated in clinical trials for cancer and AIDS. There is as yet no scientific support for the numerous claims and anecdotes that this plant can cure cancer, but there is preliminary clinical evidence that it has a direct anti-cancer effect in some cancers and that it acts as an immune stimulant. Infusion made from the leaves is a traditional remedy for fever, chicken pox, flu, rheumatism, hemorrhoids, diarrhaea, and stomach and liver problems. It also makes an excellent wash for wounds. Sunbirds pollinate the attractive, butterfly-like red flowers. The lightweight, papery, inflated pods enable the seed to be dispersed easily by wind. A rather short-lived species that is fairly common on dune strandveld on Grootbos, especially along road verges and in disturbed areas. It has a natural distribution from Namaqualand and the Western Karoo to the Eastern Cape.

① Lessertia herbacea

September   October

An annual, non-climbing herb that is erect or ascending, with scattered, sharp-pointed, straight, stiff hairs lying flat on the leaf surface. Its leaves are 55–95 mm long, few and distant, 19–30 mm apart, divided into 5–8 pairs of leaflets, often infolded, narrow-linear, rounded or with a shallow notch on a rounded apex, hairless above, with scattered, sharp-pointed, straight and stiff hairs beneath. The inflorescence stalks are often much longer than the leaves. The inflorescence is a loose raceme with many purple flowers. Its natural distribution is from the Northern Cape to the Agulhas Plain and Eastern Cape. Flowers are bird-pollinated and fruits are wind-dispersed. One of only a few *Lessertia* species that have been reported by farmers to be palatable for sheep grazing,

② Lessertia miniata

September   October

A prostrate shrublet with narrow, linear to oblong leaves. It has orange-red flowers and ellipsoid, inflated pods that are leathery or woody. It grows in coastal or limestone fynbos from the Cape Peninsula to Stilbaai.

③ Liparia splendens
subsp. splendens
mountain dahlia, skaamblom

January   March to

An erect or creeping, resprouting shrub with elliptical leaves and bearing beautiful heads of 15–17 orange to red flowers. The flowers are 35–40 mm long and are surrounded by conspicuous, dark reddish-brown bracts. It flowers profusely after fire and to a lesser extent between fires. *Liparia splendens* is visited by both sunbirds and carpenter bees in search of nectar, the pollinator being the sunbird. When the sunbird pushes its head between the petals to get to the nectar, it causes the stamens and style to pop out from the enclosing keel petals, which puts the pollen-bearing anthers and the stigma in contact with the bird's throat feathers. *Liparia* seeds have a fleshy collar-like aril that attracts ants that disperse the seeds underground. On Grootbos it is restricted to the upper sandstone slopes and there is a large population near the summit of Witkransberg. It has a natural distribution from the Cape Peninsula to Mossel Bay.

Fynbos plants have developed different strategies to survive fires, the main two being reseeding and resprouting. *Liparia splendens* is a resprouter. When a fire burns through a population the above ground parts are killed but the large underground rootstock, known as a lignotuber, survives and sends out vigorous new growth soon after the fire. Resprouters are usually multi-stemmed at ground level. Reseeders are usually single-stemmed at ground level and the whole plant is killed by the fire, but they produce large amounts of seed that germinate *en masse* after a fire.

1 **Otholobium bracteolatum**

April   November to

A sprawling shrub with 3-foliolate leaves and symmetrical, glandular, wedge-shaped leaflets. It bears dense spikes of blue, white and violet flowers 8–10 mm long. The calyx is soft-haired, glandular, with the lower sepal being the largest. It grows on coastal strandveld and limestone hills from Saldanha Bay to Grahamstown.

2 **Otholobium virgatum**

November

A trailing, resprouting plant with 3-foliolate leaves and hairless, egg-shaped leaflets. The flowers are pale pink to mauve-purple and the calyx is softly hairy with the lowest sepal being the largest. It grows in marshes and wet places from Porterville and Saldanha Bay to the Eastern Cape.

3 **Podalyria myrtillifolia**

July   September

A rounded, single-stemmed or occasionally resprouting shrub with oval to paddle-shaped leaves 10–20 x 5–10 mm that are silky on both sides. It bears pink flowers 10–16 mm long that have lance-shaped bracts. It grows on sandstone, limestone and shale flats from Tulbagh to Port Elizabeth.

4 **Psoralea arborea**
fountainbush

June   October

A small tree with deeply divided leaves that are 5–7 foliolate. It has mauve and blue sweetly scented flowers that occur in clusters towards the ends of branches. It is restricted to damp areas from Gansbaai to Humansdorp.

5 **Psoralea restioides**

August   September

A soft, rush-like plant with needle-like leaves to 30 mm long. It bears solitary blue and white flowers on 10 cm long flowering stalks. A species that grows in marshy areas in mountain and lowland fynbos from the Cape Peninsula to Bredasdorp.

The other Psoralea recorded on Grootbos is *P. aphylla* with small scale-like leaves that make the willowy branches appear leafless.

1 Rafnia triflora

A robust shrub with large, oval, usually paired leaves that turn black when dried. It has bright yellow flowers (25 mm long) that occur three at a time in the axils of the leaves. It occurs between sea level and 600 m on stony slopes from Clanwilliam to Humansdorp.

Rafnia triflora is one of the species on Grootbos that is pollinated by carpenter bees. These large bees, often mistaken for bumble bees, are solitary wood mining bees belonging to the genus *Xylocopa*. They make their nests in the dry wood of dead shrubs, particularly enjoying the dead trunks of burnt out Proteas. They are important pollinators of various fynbos species including a number of *Polygala*, *Aspalathus* and several orchids.

2 Tephrosia capensis
fish bean

A trailing, straggly perennial with sparse compound leaves on 20 mm long stalks with a swollen base. Each leaf consists of 3–6 pairs of oval leaflets that are about 20 mm long and have pointed tips. The pink to rose-red flowers occur at the end of the stems. The pods are straight, opaque, woody and hairy with numerous seeds. It occurs on the coastal dunes to inland mountain slopes on a wide variety of soils from the Cape Peninsula through the Eastern Cape to Gauteng.

3 Muraltia filiformis

A slender, hairless shrublet that branches at the base, with solitary or tufted, needle-like to narrowly lance-shaped leaves that have minute points. It bears sessile, pink flowers and produces horned fruits. A species of sandy flats, often in damp places from the Cape Peninsula to Agulhas.

4 Muraltia satureioides

An erect or spreading shrub with hairy young stems. It has crowded branches of oblong leaves that are 3–8 mm long and spine-tipped when young. It bears white or pink flowers on short pedicels and produces fruits that are stiff-haired and prominently horned. It grows on dune fynbos and limestone between the Cape Peninsula and Knysna.

① Muraltia spinosa
tortoise berry

June   July

(=*Nylandtia spinosa*) A spiny, rounded shrub that is sparsely covered with small, narrow pungent leaves between 3–6 mm long. The numerous pink to purple flowers produce round, red, fleshy fruits that are a favourite for tortoises, birds and people during the summer. It was first illustrated in 1685 during Simon van der Stel's expedition to Namaqualand, and was reported to be thirst quenching. It is rich in Vitamin C. An infusion of the leaves is made to treat colds, flu and bronchitis. It grows on sandy flats and slopes from Namaqualand to the Eastern Cape.

Other Muraltia on Grootbos are the dune strandveld species, *M. bolusii* branching at the base with axillary pink flowers 3–4 mm long and *M. stipulacea* with leaves that are hairy below, spine-tipped and the calyx is more than half as long as the corolla; the limestone species, *M. salsolacea* with oval to linear, spine-tipped leaves and the mountain fynbos species *M. divaricata* with linear leaves and hairy young stems, the glabrescent *M. ericoides* with solitary, sessile linear to oval leaves, the erect *M. heisteria* with channelled, ciliate leaves that are spine tipped and *M. filiformis* with needle-like leaves of damper sandstone slopes.

② Polygala myrtifolia
September bush

All year

A sturdy, large bush with variable bright green leaves. It has magenta, pink or occasionally white, pale-crested flowers up to 22 mm long that are in short terminal racemes. It occurs in coastal scrub and forest margins fron Vanrhynsdorp to the Transkei. A beautiful garden plant, that blooms all year and is well adapted for coastal fynbos gardening.

③ Polygala bracteolata

August   November

A lax or erect perennial that branches mostly at the base. It has lance-shaped narrow leaves that are up to 30 mm long. The pink, magenta or rarely white flowers are 12–19 mm long and borne in crowded clusters at the ends of the main branches. The flowers have a white, brush-like crest and are pollinated by carpenter bees. The side petals are hairy below with a large lower lobe. It grows from Vanrhynsdorp to Humansdorp from sea level to 900 m.

Other Polygala on Grootbos are the limestone and dune strandveld species, the 20 cm high, sprawling *P. dasyphylla* (endangered) with pink flowers in crowded, terminal heads, the closely leafy *P. meridionalis* with purple flowers and the stiffly branched *P. pubiflora* with oval-shaped leaves that are heart-shaped at the base, and the mountain species: the sprawling *P. scabra* with linear to lance-shaped leaves with revolute margins and few purple flowers in slender, axillary racemes, *P. umbellata* with sprawling branches from a woody base and *P. uncinata* with ascending, linear leaves with rolled margins and purple flowers in terminal racemes.

1 Cliffortia anthospermoides

August   October

An erect shrub with reddish young branches and long white hairs turning greyish brown and smooth as they age. As the stems further mature, the bark splits and peels, leaving a smooth, glabrous reddish-brown surface. It has bright green, trifoliate leaves, the leaflets 5.5–7 x 0.9–1 mm, straight to sickle-shaped to twisted with scabrid margins. The leaves are tightly packed on the stem and alternate. The flowers are solitary in the axils of leaves. While the male and female flowers are produced on the same plant, they are produced at different times. The female flowers, with their showy red styles are the first to appear on the plant. The male phase follows – characterised by its showy maroon stamens. At first sight this species can be easily mistaken for a member of the genus Anthospermum (Rubiaceae), hence the name given to the plant. The tightly packed leaves obscure their alternate arrangement on the stem which would distinguish a non-flowering specimen from being an Anthospermum. The species grows on sandy, alkaline soils on slight slopes and is only known from the Gansbaai area. A total of only four populations have ever been recorded. The population at Woeste Arabie between Stanford and Grootbos was destroyed by road widening, the one at Danger Point is threatened by coastal development and the one at Wortelgat has been severely impacted by dense stands of *Acacia cyclops*. From a conservation perspective the only population that has a secure future is the one on the lower slopes near the Grootbos Lodges.

2 Cliffortia ilicifolia
doringtee

March   December

An erect shrub with simple, oval flat leaves that have hard, spiny teeth on their margins. As its name suggests, the leaves of this species were traditionally utilised as a tea substitute. It grows on damp sandstone slopes between the Cape Peninsula and Port Elizabeth.

3 Cliffortia falcata

April   July

A compact shrub with both sexes on one plant or on separate plants. It has trifoliolate leaves, with 6–12 mm long leaflets that are sickle-shaped and have margins that are rolled backwards. It grows on coastal slopes from the Cape Peninsula to Knysna.

4 Cliffortia ferruginea
glastee

July   November to

A sprawling shrublet with reddish branches and glossy leaves that creep along the ground in wet areas. It has linear to oval-shaped leaves with margins edged with tooth-like projections. The leaf apex is coarsely toothed and curved to one side. This species is popular amongst indigenous gardeners as a glossy groundcover, especially around water. It grows naturally from the Cape Peninsula to Port Elizabeth, usually on lower damp slopes.

❶ Cliffortia stricta

June   October to

A compact shrub, with both sexes on one plant or on separate plants. It has trifoliolate leaves with large, conspicuous brown sheaths and stipules. The leaflets are linear, hairy and 4–8 mm long. The male flowers have six stamens and the female receptacle is smooth and 12-veined. It grows on flats and lower slopes between the Cape Peninsula and Humansdorp.

Other Cliffortia on Grootbos are *C. filifolia* with fine, needle-like, slightly curved leaves on lower slopes, *C. obcordata* with flat leaflets, the central heart-shaped and the lateral egg-shaped also on lower slopes, *C. phyllanthoides* with bifoliolate leaves, leaflets flat and heart-shaped and the tall *C. strobilifera* to 3 m, often bearing cone-shaped galls and having simple, linear leaves.

26. RHAMNACEAE

Phylica family

❷ Phylica dodii

April   September

A low, resprouting, wiry shrub, with reddish branches that bear closely-set linear, smooth leaves (8–20 mm long) with margins curved downwards. The whitish flowers are solitary in rounded heads that are surrounded by many hairy leaves with enlarged petioles. It grows in sandy habitats from the Cape Peninsula to Knysna.

❸ Phylica ericoides

All year

A compact, much-branched shrub with narrow, often rough, ericoid leaves about 8 mm long. It bears minute flowers that are densely crowded together in white, rounded posy heads about 4–7 mm across. The heads are often massed towards the tips of the branches. It grows on dunes and lower slopes from the Cape Peninsula to the Eastern Cape and southern tropical Africa.

❹ Phylica imberbis

April   November to

A closely leafy, loosely branched shrub with linear leaves, 7–10 mm long that are smooth except on the edges. The leaf margins are rolled down and inwards. It bears flowers in mostly solitary, rounded heads and grows on sandstone slopes on the Reserve. It is a widespread species growing on sandstone slopes and flats from the Bokkeveld Mountains to Knysna and the Swartberg Mountains.

The much-branched, hairy *P. axillaris* has flowers well below branch tips that flower from December to April and *P. disticha* with flowers in small, usually flattened heads have also been recorded on Grootbos.

❶ Trichocephalus stipularis
dogface

A resprouting shrub with many stems arising from a persistent rootstock. The edges of the alternate, narrow leaves are rolled under and there is a pair of dry red stipules at either side of the base. The flowers are pink and are tightly massed into woolly honey scented heads. Usually only three flowers per head produce capsules. A common species of sandy flats and lowland slopes from the Cederberg to Knysna.

27. URTICACEAE

Nettle family

❷ Droguetia iners

A softly woody perennial with male and female flowers on separate plants. It has soft, mostly opposite leaves that are lance-shaped and toothed, with the apical tooth longer than wide. It produces small clusters of greenish flowers at the ends of branches. This species is very common in the shade of the milkwood forest. While for many it looks like a stinging nettle, this species is fortunately a rather tame, stingless, member of the nettle family! It grows from the Cape Peninsula to Indonesia.

28. MYRICACEAE

Waxberry family

❸ Morella quercifolia
maagpynbossie

An erect shrub with a fire-resistant rootstock. It has lobed leaves about 20 mm long that are similar to the leaves of oak trees, hence the Latin name *quercifolia*. The yellowish flowers are arranged on hanging catkins. It is reputed to cure stomach cramps. It grows on sandy flats and slopes between Malmesbury and Uitenhage, as well as in Namaqualand and Transkei.

❹ Morella cordifolia
wax berry

A straggling shrub with overlapping, stalkless, heart-shaped, toothed leaves that are 5–10 mm long and 5–8 mm in diameter. It produces greyish, warty fruits on spikes at the end of branches. The coating of the fruits was once used for making domestic candles and furniture polish. It is a coastal species that is an important dune stabiliser and grows from Yzerfontein to the Eastern Cape.

① Kedrostis nana
porcupine potato

February — March

A tuberous perennial climber with male and female flowers on separate plants. It has slightly lobed leaves and greenish flowers at end of stems. The fruits are berry-like and the tubers are a favourite food for porcupines. It grows in coastal scrub from Saldanha Bay to KwaZulu-Natal.

The creeper *Zehneria scabra* with cordate leaves that are rough above and softly hairy below and has cream-coloured flowers is also found in the milkwood forests on the Reserve.

30. CELASTRACEAE

Staff vine or bittersweet family

② Cassine peragua
bastard saffronwood

   to 10m

January — June

A large bush or small tree, with leathery, almost circular leaves 70–100 mm long that have irregularly serrated margins. It has loose clusters of small, cream flowers that produce purplish-black, fleshy fruits, much loved by birds. While it can grow as a single-stemmed tree, it is usually found as a multi-stemmed bush in coastal fynbos and thicket having resprouted following fires. It has characteristic orange bark and grows between the Cape Peninsula and Mpumalanga.

③ Pterocelastrus tricuspidatus
cherrywood, kershout

April — July

A small tree with oval, thick, leathery leaves about 50 mm long that are shiny above and pale green below. The leaves have a shallow-notched point and the margins are slightly rolled under. The young leaves are faintly veined and the leaf stalks are pink-red. The small, fragrant flowers are creamy-white to yellowish and occur in compact clusters. The orange-yellow capsular fruits have three lobes, each with characteristic two-winged 'horns'. It occurs in dune fynbos, coastal thickets and mountain forests between the Cape Peninsula and Mpumalanga.

④ Robsonodendron maritimum
duine-sybas

June — October

A low, rigid dense shrub with spreading branches and angular green twigs. The thick, slightly fleshy leaves are about 70 mm long. It has small white to cream-coloured flowers and produces white fruits. It grows in dune fynbos and on thicket margins between the Cape Peninsula and Port Elizabeth.

1 Oxalis depressa
March April

A geophyte with a shallow bulb and trifoliolate leaves that have wedge-shaped, succulent leaflets and large epidermal cells. It produces white, lilac or pink flowers with yellow tubes and grows naturally over a large area from the Cold Bokkeveld to Zimbabwe.

2 Oxalis luteola
sandsuring
May August

A dwarf plant with basal, three-lobed, hairy leaves that are notched at the tips and conspicuously veined beneath. It has bright yellow flowers that are borne singly on jointed stalks which, after flowering, arch over to bring the developing seeds near to the ground. It is the only yellow-flowered species in this area with a ground-hugging rosette of leaves. It grows on sandy flats and lower slopes between Clanwilliam and Riversdale.

3 Oxalis obtusa
geeloogsuring
June October

A stemless perennial with leaves divided into three broadly wedge- or heart-shaped leaflets that are hairless or hairy. It bears pink, brick-red, yellow or white flowers with darker veins and a yellow tube on jointed flower stems that are covered with downward-facing hairs. It is widespread and common occuring from Namaqualand to the Eastern Cape.

4 Oxalis pardalis
May June

A geophyte with trifoliolate leaves that are linear to elliptic in shape and smooth or hairy. The flowers are orange, red-purple, pink, yellow, white or cream-coloured, with a yellow tube. It is usually found in heavier soils between 150 and 600 m above sea level and grows from the Bokkeveld Mountains through the Karoo to Mossel Bay.

5 Oxalis pes-caprae
geelsuring
June October

A stemless perennial with basal, three-lobed leaves consisting of heart-shaped leaflets that are hairless above and hairy beneath. The canary yellow flowers occur in loose clusters of 3–20 at the ends of long stems. This is a common plant, traditionally enjoyed by children who suck out the sour juices from the bottom of the stem. It grows from Namaqualand to Humansdorp.

❶ Oxalis stellata

April — June

A geophyte with a beaked bulb. It has terminal leaves that are trifoliolate, the leaflets are deeply bilobed. It has 3–6 rosy or white flowers with a yellow tube per flowering stalk. It grows from the Cape Peninsula to Port Elizabeth.

Other Oxalis recorded on Grootbos are *Oxalis caprina* with a very short to absent stem and pale lilac or white flowers with a greenish tube, *O. glabra* with a small bulb and spreading by runners to form dense carpets, *O. lindaviana* with white flowers and greenish throats and growing on rocky south-facing slopes, *O. polyphylla* with its leaves divided into 3(7) thread-like, folded leaflets, *O. purpurea* with leaves that have purple under surfaces and hairy margins and *O. zeekoevleyensis* with heart-shaped leaves that are sparsely hairy beneath and rosy lilac flowers with yellow tubes.

32. EUPHORBIACEAE

Rubber tree, spurge and milkweed family

❷ Clutia alaternoides
jeukbossie

February — June

A hairless, resprouting shrub with sessile oval leaves with toothed margins and a fine pointed tip. The cream-coloured female flowers are borne singly in the leaf axils and produce round hairless 3-chambered capsules. The 4 mm long clustered male flowers are borne on separate plants and emerge beyond the leaves. This is a common species on the lower sandy flats on Grootbos and has a natural distribution from Namaqualand to Port Elizabeth.

Clutia ericoides has distinctly concave leaves, black axillary buds and cream flowers while the similar *C. polygonoides* has leathery, almost stalkless leaves that are narrow, oblong and 12–18 mm long and grows on the sandstone slopes of the Reserve.

❸ Euphorbia tuberosa
melkbol

April — September

A dwarf, tuberous geophyte with a basal rosette of strap-shaped, spreading leaves with wavy edges. The leaves and flowering stem produce a milky latex. It produces loose clusters of yellow-green, cup-shaped flowers on longish, lax stems. It occurs from Vanrhynsdorp to the Cape Peninsula and the Agulhas Plain

The only other Euphorbia recorded on Grootbos is *E. erythrina* which is easily distinguishable by its 600 mm tall stem covered with small, oval leaves. It produces copious amounts of white milky juice when damaged.

33. LINACEAE

1 Linum africanum

January — September to

A perennial with slender stems that is able to resprout from a persistent woody base after fire. It has narrow, lance-shaped leaves with small glands near their base and bears loose panicles of yellow flowers that are reddish below. It grows on sandstone and limestone slopes and flats from Hopefield to Knysna.

34. VIOLACEAE

Violet family

2 Viola decumbens
wild violet

July — December

A slender, often woody shrublet, which can form cushion-like bushes or scramble between the undergrowth. It has linear leaves and bears nodding, faintly-scented, blue-violet flowers that have a tubular spur. It is related to the pansy, *Viola odorata*, and the heartsease, *Viola tricolor*, which are popular garden plants. It grows on damp sandstone slopes from the Cape Peninsula to Bredasdorp.

35. GERANIACEAE

Geranium family

The well-known Geraniums cultivated around the world are artificial hybrids of the South African genus Pelargonium. The beauty and diversity of the Pelargoniums of the Cape attracted the attention of early travellers and plants were already being brought to Europe in the early years of the 17th century to be planted in estate gardens. Certain species of Pelargonium yield geranium oil which contains geraniol and citronellol, substitutes for the expensive attar of roses in the perfume industry. Pelargoniums are cultivated in the Cape as well as around the world for these oils. A total of 12 species of Pelargonium and two species of Geranium have been recorded on Grootbos.

3 Geranium incanum
bergtee, vrouebossie

August — October

An attractive, sprawling perennial shrublet with finely divided silvery leaves. The white, pale pink, violet or magenta flowers are borne on long, slender stalks, followed by characteristically elongated fruit resembling a stork's bill. The flowers are about 25 mm wide and the petals are notched at the tips. The leaves have traditionally been utilised to make a traditional tea (bergtee), which was used for treating bladder infections and menstruation-related ailments, hence the common name vrouebossie ('vroue' = women; 'bossie' = small bush). It grows on sandy and stony grounds from the Cape Peninsula to Port Alfred.

❶ Geranium ornithopodon

    February   October to

A clump-forming perennial with a thick, woody rootstock. The leaves are hand-like, five-lobed with the lobes starting more than half way to the base of the sparsely haired leaves. It usually produces two flowers on long flowering stems that are 15–20 mm wide and pale pink with darker veins or entirely white. It grows on damp ground in scrub or forest margins from the Cape Peninsula to the Eastern Cape.

❷ Pelargonium alchemilloides
lady's mantle-leaved pelargonium

    September   November

A sprawling perennial that sprouts from a woody rootstock. It has round leaves that are usually lobed, about 7 mm in diameter, and often with reddish zonal marking and sparse silky hairs. The stipules are broadly oval shaped. The white, yellow or pink flowers are borne in spring. A decoction of the root is used in Lesotho to bathe a feverish patient. It grows in moist places from Saldanha Bay to the Northern Province. It is often found in disturbed places.

❸ Pelargonium betulinum
maagpynbossie

   August   October

An erect or sprawling shrub with leaves that are hard and have uneven red-tipped teeth on their margins. The flowerheads comprise clusters of one to six flowers that are pink to mauve with dark streaks. The upper two petals are broader and darker coloured than the lower three. Its striking flowerheads and adaptation to coastal conditions make it an excellent species for coastal indigenous gardening. The vapour from steaming the leaves has been used traditionally to treat coughs and other chest problems. It has also been used to treat stomachaches. It occurs on coastal dunes and limestone from Yzerfontein to Knysna.

❹ Pelargonium capitatum
coastal malva, wild rose geranium

   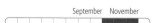 September   October

A sprawling shrublet with heart-shaped, lobed, hairy aromatic leaves about 50 mm wide. The purple-pink flowers, with beetroot-purple stripes on the upper petals, are grouped together 8 –20 in a tight cluster that is raised above the leaves on sturdy erect stalks. It is a natural skin softener and the sweetly scented leaves can be rubbed into hands to soothe callouses and scratches, or into the heels to soften cracked skin. The leaves can also be tied into a piece of cloth and used in the bath as a wash and skin treatment and to soothe rashes. It is an important pioneer species and grows naturally on coastal sands from Lamberts Bay to KwaZulu-Natal.

❶ Pelargonium cucullatum
wild malva

  February   September to

A sturdy large shrub that becomes woody at the base, but with hairy soft new growth. It has kidney-shaped, aromatic, 45 mm long leaves that are cupped and pleated with irregular, sometimes reddish edges. The flowerheads comprise 4–10 large flowers that are usually pink to purple with dark red veins on the upper two petals. It is an excellent fast growing plant for indigenous landscaping and restoration projects, that grows best on sandstone soils although it will tolerate alkaline sands. It grows naturally on coastal flats and lower slopes between Saldanha Bay and Baardskeerdersbos.

❷ Pelargonium elegans

  January   September to

A tufted shrublet with tough, orb-shaped leaves (20–40 mm wide) that have coarsely toothed, hairy margins and are borne at the end of long stalks. The branching flowering stalk usually bears two to four (up to seven) flowers that are pale pink to lilac, with dark purple veins on the two upper petals. It is a stoloniferous species meaning the majority of plants in a population are connected by underground stolons. It occurs on coastal dunes and flats from Hermanus to Grahamstown.

❸ Pelargonium grossularioides
gooseberry-leaved pelargonium

   All year

A low, spreading annual with long, reddish stems, branching from the base. Individual stems may reach a length of 50 cm and are characterised by long, angular and furrowed reddish internodes. The stems and leaves are aromatic and glabrous to fairly hairy. It has heart-shaped, purplish, 50 x 40 mm leaves. The upper leaves are usually much smaller and more deeply incised. Triangular stipules are found at the base of the long, reddish leaf stalks. The purple flowers are about 8 mm in diameter, relatively inconspicuous and borne in 3–50 flowered compact heads. It is a species of damp places from Clanwilliam to KwaZulu-Natal.

❹ Pelargonium longifolium
bearded pelargonium

  October   December

A tuberous geophyte with an underground, cylindrical or oval-shaped tuber. Its leaves vary considerably, even on the same plant. Leaf blades are linear, lance-shaped, or oval with entire margins. They can also be shallowly to deeply incised. The length of the leaf blades varies from 1–12 cm and the width from 3–70 mm. The flowering stems are hairy and branched bearing 3–9-flowered heads. The colour of the petals varies from white to pink with dark purple markings. It grows in sandy or rocky places from Calvinia to Port Elizabeth.

❶ Pelargonium myrrhifolium
myrrh-leaved pelargonium

 to 30cm | February — August to

A soft, hairy shrublet with weak stems that bear deeply divided leaves that are about 80 mm long, including the long leafstalk. It bears up to five white or pale pink flowers that are carried well above the leaves. The upper petals are much larger than the lower petals, and have carmine nectar guides. This species has its nectar hidden at the base of a deep tube which closely matches the length of a large grey fly with a proboscis up to 40 mm long. It grows in open places between Clanwilliam and Willowmore.

P. myrrhifolium var. coriandrifolium is also found on Grootbos and can be distinguished by its more finely divided leaves.

❷ Pelargonium suburbanum
  to 30cm | January — June to

A sprawling shrublet with divided leaves that are 3–7 mm in diameter. It produces cream to purple flowers, with the two upper petals being much wider than the lower petals. It grows on coastal dunes from the Cape Peninsula to Port Elizabeth.

❸ Pelargonium triste
kaneelbol, rooiwortel

   to 50cm | February — August to

A tuberous species that has hairy, dissected leaves 100 to 450 mm long. The flowerhead of 6–20 flowers is borne at the end of a long, hairy stalk. The flowers have yellowish-green to brown-purple petals edged with a lighter margin and emit a musk scent at night. Its roots were traditionally used to treat diarrhoea and dysentery. It occurs on sandy or gravelly flats and lower slopes from Clanwilliam to Uniondale.

Other Pelargoniums recorded on Grootbos are *P. fergusoniae*, a tuberous geophyte with palmate leaves dry at flowering time and the scrambling *P. hypoleucum* of cool slopes with white to pink flowers.

36. PENAEACEAE

Penaea family

❹ Penaea mucronata
 to 1m | February — September to

An erect shrub, coppicing from a woody base, with closely overlapping heart- to lance-shaped leaves about 8 mm long that have pointed tips. The tubular, yellow to reddish flowers occur in clumps at the tips of branches. It is a common and widespread species on sandstone slopes from the Cape Peninsula to the Langeberg.

❶ Searsia glauca
blue kuni-bush

(= *Rhus glauca*) A tough, much-branched shrub to small tree with trifoliolate leaves that often have a bluish-green colour. The greenish white flowers are borne in loose clusters and the round, shiny fruit are bluish dark brown. This widespread species grows mostly on dunes between Veldrift and Kentani in the Eastern Cape.

❷ Searsia laevigata
dune taaibos

(= *Rhus laevigata*) A deciduous shrub with male and female flowers on separate plants. It has trifoliolate leaves, the leaflets being sessile, egg-shaped, glossy or hairy. The flowers are greenish yellow and the fruits are round and shiny. Traditionally the leaves, bark and roots were used medicinally. Leaves were chewed for chest colds, the roots are claimed to be of therapeutic value in infective disorders of the gastro-intestinal tract. It grows on coastal flats and slopes between Lamberts Bay and East London.

❸ Searsia lucida
blinktaaibos

(= *Rhus lucida*) An evergreen shrub that can coppice after fire and is often multi-stemmed from the ground. It has shiny green, trifoliolate leaves; the leaflets are sessile and egg-shaped. It produces yellow flowers and round, shiny fruits. A species of sandy flats and slopes between Citrusdal and Zimbabwe.

❹ Searsia rosmarinifolia
rosemary, taaibos

(= *Rhus rosmarinifolia*) A straggling shrublet, with trifoliate leaves, the straight to curved narrow leaflets are wrinkled and greyish green above and white below. It has cream flowers that are borne in clusters, each flower borne on a separate stalk. The male and female flowers are borne on separate plants. The oblong fruits are woolly. It grows in rocky soils in fynbos between Clanwilliam and Port Elizabeth.

Other Searsia on Grootbos are *Searsia crenata* with wavy-toothed margins, and *S. tomentosa* with toothed leaflets that are whiter on the underside (see page 280).

The citrus family, Rutaceae, have oil-bearing glands on their leaves. The best known genus in the family is Agathosma, locally known as buchu. This genus comprises 143 species (96% endemic to the fynbos region). When buchu leaves are crushed, the strongly-scented oils are released, delightful to smell in the case of some species and less so in the case of others. Bushmen and Khoi pastoralists mixed dried and powdered leaves with sheep fat to anoint their bodies for cosmetic and insect-repellent purposes (freshly crushed buchu leaves wiped across exposed skin is a great way of deterring troublesome horseflies and ticks). They also chewed the leaves of some species to relieve stomach complaints. Dutch settlers quickly learnt of the medicinal value of buchu: they imbibed concoctions of buchu leaves and vinegar or brandy, and buchu tea as treatments for stomach complaints, worms, and kidney and bladder ailments. This traditional knowledge underpins the multi-million rand buchu industry of today.

❶ Agathosma abrupta

April — August

A single-stemmed, much branched, tangled shrublet that has hairy, scarcely aromatic leaves. It has white or pale pink flowers in clusters at the axils of the branches or at the end of the branches. It is a local endemic species that grows on limestone outcrops between Grootbos and Hagelkraal.

❷ Agathosma cerefolium
anysboegoe, beach buchu

January — August to

A single-stemmed shrublet with strongly aniseed-scented, needle-like to rounded leaves (3–5 mm long) that are hairy on the margins and vary from slightly concave to convex above. It bears loose clusters of white, pink or mauve flowers with petals 3–5 mm long and lance-shaped staminodes. This species is used in cosmetics, soaps and perfumes. It also makes a lovely addition to pot-pourris. It is found on limestone soils on Grootbos and is restricted to the coastal region from Hermanus to Humansdorp.

❸ Agathosma geniculata

July — December

A rigid, resprouting shrublet with faintly pine-scented, imbricate leaves with tips pointed upwards and pale-brown to yellowish stems. The white or pale pink flowers are in dense terminal clusters. This species is rare on Grootbos, where it is found on limestone and has a very restricted distribution on limestone between Stanford and Stilbaai.

❶ Agathosma imbricata

January   July to

wildeboegoe

A resprouting shrub with sweetly or herb-scented, lance-shaped to rounded leaves 2.5–5 mm long, concave above and with hairy margins. It bears dense clusters of white, pink or purple (most common on Grootbos) flowers with petals 4–7.5 mm long and spoon-shaped staminodes. It is widespread in the southwestern and southern Cape from Tulbagh to Knysna.

❷ Agathosma serpyllacea

May   December

A single-stemmed shrublet with needle-like to lance-shaped leaves that are distinctly swollen behind their tips and slightly twisted, mostly 5–10 mm long. It bears clusters of white, pink or purple flowers with petals 3.5–5.5 mm long and with peg-like or lance-shaped staminodes. This species is the most common buchu on Grootbos and is particularly common on the slopes behind Garden Lodge. It occurs on coastal or inland sand or limestone flats from Piketberg to Humansdorp.

A. ciliaris is a dense, rounded shrublet to 45 cm that is aniseed scented and found on sandstone soils on Grootbos and sometimes roots where its stem becomes buried.

❸ Diosma hirsuta

July   November

rooiboegoe

A resprouting shrublet coppicing from a woody rootstock after fire with aromatic, sharply-pointed, needle-like leaves 10–22 mm long x 1 mm wide. It bears short racemes of white flowers that are grouped at the branch tips, with petals persisting below the fruits. It occurs on sandstone and clay slopes from the Cederberg to Humansdorp.

❹ Diosma subulata

March   November

A tall single-stemmed shrub with opposite, erect, needle like or lance-shaped incurved leaves 5–17 x 2–3 mm wide with a pungent aroma. It bears small clusters of white flowers at the end of its branches. This species is restricted to dune sands and is common on the deep sands around the Grootbos Milkwood forest. It occurs naturally from Hawston to Cape Agulhas.

The vulnerable *Diosma awilana* is like *D. subulata* but has alternate, sessile leaves with recurved tips and is found on limestones on Grootbos.

❶ Anisodontea scabrosa
sandroos

   All year

An erect, much branched, often sticky and aromatic shrub. It has coarsely toothed, rough leaves that are variable in shape, the lower 20–70 mm long but much reduced in size amongst the flowers. The red to pinkish to off-white flowers are hibiscus-like and occur singly or in small groups in the axils of the leaves. It is widespread in coastal areas from Saldanha Bay to Port Elizabeth as well as elsewhere in southern Africa.

❷ Hermannia hyssopifolia
pokkiesblom

  September October

A greyish, twiggy shrub with wedge-shaped leaves that are toothed above. It bears dense terminal clusters of cream to pale yellow flowers with a pin-hole throat and much swollen, urn-shaped papery calyx. It grows on granite, sandstone and clay slopes from the Cape Peninsula to the Eastern Cape.

❸ Hermannia joubertiana

  September October

A sparsely branched, often hairless shrublet with inversely lance-shaped to wedge-shaped leaves that are usually sparsely toothed above. Its small, golden-yellow flowers are on slender flower stalks and grouped in tight clusters. It grows on limestone soils form Hermanus to Mossel Bay.

❹ Hermannia scabricaulis

   August September

A glandular-hairy, prostrate shrublet with oval-shaped, irregularly lacerated leaves on petioles. It produces two or three orange to red, bell-shaped flowers on axillary and terminal peduncles. The fruiting capsules are large, oblong and inflated. It grows on coastal sands and limestone from the Cape Peninsula to De Hoop.

❺ Hermannia ternifolia
tandebossie

  September November

A prostrate or sprawling shrublet with small, slightly toothed, grey, velvety leaves. It has small, pin-wheel flowers that are yellow tinged with orange-red. It grows on sand dunes and coastal limestone from Saldanha Bay to the Agulhas Plain.

1 ## Hermannia trifoliata

August — September

A sprawling shrublet with stiffly erect, grey, velvety, reflexed leaves. The leaves are often sessile and densely arranged, overlapping along the stem. It has orange to red pin-wheel flowers with an inflated calyx in terminal clusters and is confined to limestone soils from Hermanus to the Gouritzmond.

2 ## Hibiscus aethiopicus

February — June to

A sprawling subshrub that sprouts from a woody rootstock. It has oval to elliptical leaves that are sometimes coarsely toothed at the ends, 3–5 veined from the base and hairy beneath but almost hairless above. It bears cream to yellow flowers in the axils, often with dark centres. It grows on damp sandstone or clay slopes from the Elandskloof Mountains to KwaZulu-Natal.

The annual, *Hibiscus trionium* with its yellow flower and a dark eye is another wetland species recorded on Grootbos.

40. THYMELAEACEAE

Daphne or stripbark family

This family of plants is easy to identify as all its members have bark that strips. The tubular flowers of most species are fragrant at night and adapted to moth pollination. The common name daphne family refers to the early usage of the yellow flowers of Gnidia deserticola as a source of dye for leather. The tough, fibrous bark that characteristically comes off in long strips has traditionally been utilised to make rope.

3 ## Gnidia juniperifolia

All year

An erect or spreading shrublet with scattered leaves. It produces pairs of unscented, yellow flowers at the end of the branches with a hairless, funnel-shaped tube and four membranous petal-like scales at the mouth. The leaves around the flowers are slightly broader than elsewhere on the plant. It grows on mountain slopes from the Cape Peninsula to Riversdale.

4 ## Gnidia squarrosa

June — October

A much-branched willowy shrub with narrow lance-shaped leaves, 8 mm long and 1 mm wide. The plant is characterised by masses of creamy-green to yellow flowers in late winter and spring. The flowers have a fine-hairy 7 mm long tube and eight finger-like petals in the mouth.

They have a sweet scent in the evenings. It is found growing on limestone and dune sands from the Cape Peninsula to KwaZulu-Natal.

① Gnidia tenella

  to 2m

May   November

A lax shrub with beautiful, alternate, hairy, silvery leaves. The small, creamy yellow flowers have a well developed tube with four petals that are grouped in 2–4 at the end of the branches. It is found on neutral soils and sandstone slopes from the Cape Peninsula to Bredasdorp.

Other species of *Gnidia* found on Grootbos are *Gnidia galpinii*, a seeding shrublet to 60 cm with opposite leaves and yellow flowers paired at branch tips and the yellow flowered *G. subulata* growing in the dune strandveld.

② Passerina corymbosa
gonnabos

 to 2m

October   November

A tall shrub or small tree with linear leaves that have a hairy groove beneath and are 4–10 mm long. It has flowers in spikes with 4 mm long tubes and a slender neck. A good pioneer species that is common in open or disturbed sandy sites. The strong fibrous nature of the bark of this species made it useful for weaving into a twine/rope. It grows naturally from Tulbagh to the Eastern Cape.

③ Passerina paleacea

 to 1m

October   November

A smaller shrublet than *P. corymbosa* that has small compressed leaves, 1.5–2.5 mm long. It flowers in dense spikes, the flower tubes are 2 mm long, and the neck is absent. A coastal species found between Saldanha Bay and Agulhas.

④ Struthiola salteri

 to 80cm

All year

An erect to spreading shrublet with hairy branches and leaves in whorls of three or occasionally four. The flowers at the end of the branches are yellow to pinkish, with eight petals and have hairless flower tubes. This species is restricted to limestone between the Cape Peninsula and Agulhas.

⑤ Struthiola striata

  to 1m

June   September to

A shrub characterised by its overlapping, ribbed leaves. The 10 mm long cream, yellow or pinkish flowers are clothed in hairs on the outside and have four finger-like petals surrounded by pale bristles. It occurs on coastal flats and lower slope from the Cape Peninsula to the Eastern Cape.

1 ## Heliophila africana
bloubekkie

to 40cm
August   November

An annual herb that is often sprawling, with lance-shaped leaves that are lobed or toothed above and somewhat rough-haired. It bears blue or mauve flowers and narrow fruits between 13–100 mm long. It grows on sandy flats from Namaqualand to Swellendam.

2 ## Heliophila juncea
wild stock, blouriet

to 1m
August   December

A wand-like shrublet with narrow to oblong leaves. Its white to pink or purple flowers open along a central stalk from the bottom. The flowers have narrowly paddle-shaped petals 8–20 mm long. The fruits are discus-shaped and warty. It flowers most profusely after fire and is very variable in growth form and flower size. It grows on rocky sandstone slopes from Namaqualand to the Cape Peninsula and Eastern Cape.

3 ## Heliophila linearis
var. linearifolia

to 90cm
February   August to

A perennial that has narrow, linear, to oblongate leaves 10–30 mm long. Only the outer sepals have a short spurred tip and it produces elongated fruits 1.4–2.3 mm wide. It grows on sandy coastal flats from Langebaan to the Eastern Cape.

4 ## Heliophila linearis
var. reticulata

to 1.3cm
August   November

This sub-species has white flowers and wider, oblong to rounded more succulent leaves that are clasping at the base. All the sepals have a horn-like tip. It is restricted to the Gansbaai area, where it has only been recorded on Grootbos, Flower Valley and the Danger Point Peninsula to the south east.

Other *Heliophila* species recorded on Grootbos are *H. acuminata* and the annuals *H. bulbostyla* with divided leaves, blue flowers and growing on sandstone, *H. pusilla* with inversely lance-shaped leaves and white to mauve flowers growing on clay and stony soils and *H. subulata* with stipules like resinous granules, fleshy, lance-shaped leaves and blue, pink or mauve flowers growing on dune sands.

❶ Mystropetalon thomii
aardroos

 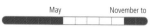

May · November to

A soft, leafless parasitic plant that produces annual above-ground stems. These consist of a dense spike of red unisexual flowers, the females on the lower and the males on the upper parts. The male flowers have spoon-shaped bracts. The seeds are dispersed by ants. It is wholly parasitic on the roots of the members of the Protea family, in particular Protea and Leucadendron. It is found infrequently in groups from the Hex River Mountains to the Cape Peninsula and eastwards to Riversdale.

Mystropetalon is a member of the Balanophoraceae family, an unusual family of parasitic flowering plants that have an aboveground inflorescence with the overall appearance of a fungus, composed of numerous minute flowers. The inflorescences develop inside the underground part of the plant, before rupturing it and surfacing. The underground portion, which attaches itself to the host, looks like a tuber, and is not a proper root system. It extracts food and water from the host plant and contains no chlorophyll.

43. SANTALACEAE

Sandalwood family

The Santalaceae are a widely distributed family of flowering plants which are partially parasitic on other plants. The green leaves contain some chlorophyll, which allows the plants to manufacture food, but all Santalaceae are parasites to a certain extent and form connections (haustoria) to their hosts to obtain water and nutrients.

❷ Colpoon speciosum

May · September to

A woody shrub that resprouts after fire from an extensive lignotuber. Following fire it develops short twiggy and leafy branches and abundant small flowers with four sepals and no petals. These produce brilliant red to purple berries that are bird dispersed. As fruiting comes to an end, buds from low on these branchlets develop into sturdy perennial branches covered in oval to elliptical leaves with thickened margins. No further flowers are produced until fire resets the cycle. It grows on the upper sandstone slopes on Grootbos and has a natural distribution from the Hottentos Holland Mountains to Bredasdorp.

❸ The much larger *Colpoon compressum* grows to 5 m and has leathery, opposite, oval to elliptic leaves with thickened margins. The greenish flowers are in delicate terminal heads and produce red to black fruits. It grows in dune strandveld.

1 Thesium commutatum   March · November to

A densely branched, nearly leafless semi-parasitic shrub. It produces leaves of two kinds. Those on the lower parts of the plant are spread out and circular in cross section, while those above are small and awl- to lance-shaped. The whitish flowers are few and crowded in terminal clusters. It grows on flats and slopes from the Koue Bokkeveld to Uitenhage.

2 Thesium spicatum   July · December
lidjiestee

A sparsely leafy, semi-parasitic shrublet with angled yellowish branches. Its leaves are terete, lie flat against the stem and have spreading tips. It produces whitish flowers in dense, oblong spikes and is most prolific in the years following fire. It grows on sandstone slopes from the Cape Peninsula to Riviersonderend Mountains.

3 Thesium strictum   February · September to
teringbos

A sparsely leafy, broom-like shrub with yellowish stems that is most healthy looking and prolific the first few years following fire. It has lance-shaped to needle-like leaves that are pressed against the stem. The whitish flowers are crowded in dense, terminal clusters. It grows on sandstone slopes from southern Namaqualand to Grahamstown.

Other *Thesium* species on Grootbos are *T. capitatum* with linear leaves, with a thickened pungent tip, the sprawling *T. capituliflorum* with lance-shaped, rounded leaves that are recurved above, the stout *T. euphrasioides* with lower linear and upper scale-like, adpressed leaves, the slender, nearly leafless *T. funale* of marshy areas, the heath-like *T. nigromontanum* with linear fleshy leaves and the densely leafy *T. scabrum* that grows to 1 m and has linear leaves with scabrid margins.

44. PLUMBAGINACEAE

Statice, plumbago and sea pink family

4 Limonium scabrum May · October to
sea lavender, statice

A branched, tufted shrublet with a basal rosette of blue-green, lance-shaped to oval leaves and sandpapery stems. The papery, lavender to violet flowers occur in a highly-branched flowerhead. It grows from the Cape Peninsula to Bredasdorp in dune and limestone fynbos as well as along rocky shores and estuaries, where it is often temporarily submerged.

❶ Drosera cistiflora
sundew, doublom

August — October

A slender, sticky perennial with an unbranched leafy stem and a basal rosette of tentacle-bearing leaves that are 20–30 mm long, and longer leaves arising from the upright stem. The white, red, yellow, purple or mauve flowers have a characteristic dark green eye. It grows on sandy slopes or temporary seeps from Namaqualand to Port Elizabeth.

❷ Drosera trinervia

August — November

A stemless, tufted perennial with red, wedge-shaped leaves in a basal rosette. It bears a few small, white to mauve or red single terminal flowers 10–16 mm in diameter. The stigmas are each divided into many branches. It grows on peaty sandstone slopes from Namaqualand to Agulhas.

The *Drosera* species or sundews grow mostly in seeps with soils that are poor in nutrients and obtain their nitrogen and phosphorous not from the soil, but from insects that they capture and devour. Their leaves are covered in glandular tentacles, each tipped with a drop of sticky fluid. Contact with one of these 'glue' drops is sufficient to make the initial capture. This is followed by rapid multiplication of cells on one side of the surrounding tentacles which then bend in towards the victim. Digestive enzymes in the glue then break down the insect and nutrients released from its body are absorbed directly into the leaf.

46. CARYOPHYLLACEAE

Carnation family

❸ Dianthus caespitosus

January — September to

A loosely tufted or spreading perennial with narrow, linear leaves about 25 mm long. It produces single white to purple flowers at the end of leafless flower stalks. The petals are always toothed or fringed. It grows on sandstone slopes from Botterkloof to Worcester and eastwards to Uitenhage.

❹ Silene undulata
wildetabak

July — September

A hairy, often sticky annual or perennial plant with pairs of pointed leaves about 200 mm long. The white or pinkish-red flowers open late afternoon and are about 300 mm wide and have bilobed petals and a long, tubular calyx. It grows in shady places amongst bushes and rocks throughout southern Africa.

1 **Pharnaceum lanatum**

August   October

A sprawling or erect shrublet that is woody at the base. The linear leaves are mostly near the base of the plant, scattered and alternately arranged. The stipules are sheathing and stipular hairs are curled, forming a woolly mass. It produces white flowers, 3-4 mm long in lax cymes on long flower stalks. It grows on sandy flats and slopes from Namaqualand to the Cape Peninsula.

2 **Pharnaceum lineare**

June   November

A sprawling perennial with elongated internodes and cylindrical leaves in whorls. The 5–8 mm long white flowers are produced at the end of long, lax, branched flowering stalks. It grows on sandy slopes and flats from Namaqualand to Bredasdorp.

48. AIZOACEAE

Vygie or mesemb family

3 **Aizoon sarmentosum**

June   October

A prostrate or spreading subshrub with leaves that are hairy and pressed to the stem when young. The leaves are mostly at the base of the plant, subterete and opposite. The white flowers are usually 1–3 but up to five at branch tips. It grows on dry flats and lower slopes from Namqualand to Montagu.

4 **Carpanthea pomeridiana**

September   November

An annual succulent with soft-haired stems and flat, slightly succulent leaves with hair-like protuberances on the margins. It bears yellow flowers with hair-like protuberances on the calyx and capsules that once ripened only release seed when wet. It grows on sandy flats from Vanrhynsdorp to Gansbaai.

5 **Carpobrotus acinaciformis**
sour fig, khoi fig

August   October

A prostrate creeper with succulent, sabre-shaped leaves up to 90 mm long and triangular in cross-section. It produces brilliant magenta flowers about 10 cm across. The leaf juice is antiseptic and traditionally gargled to treat mouth and throat infections. It is highly astringent and has traditionally been applied externally to treat excema, wounds and burns. It is also said to be effective against toothache and earache and mothers used to wipe their babies mouths with a juice-soaked cloth after lactation. It grows in sandy places from Saldanha Bay to Mossel Bay.

❶ Carpobrotus edulis
sour fig, suurvy

August   October

A mat-forming, creeper with prostrate stems up to 2 m long that can root at the nodes. The dull green fleshy leaves are 40–80 mm long and triangular in cross section. The yellow flowers fade to pinkish and produce fleshy edible fruits that are popular for making a sweet, uniquely Cape jam called *suurvy konfyt* (sour fig jam). The leaves have medicinal properties similar to those of *C. acinaciformis*. The juice of the leaves is commonly used as a

The harvesting of sour figs, derived from three species of '*Carpobrotus*' in the vygie family (Aizoaceae), comprises a small and relatively informal industry on the coastal lowlands of the fynbos region. The ripe fruits of *C. acinaciformis* are harvested in the Western Cape which supports the most extensive populations of this species; *C. deliciosus* (known locally as t'gokum or ghoukum) is harvested in the southern and eastern coasts; and *C. edulis* is harvested throughout the region.

lotion for bluebottle stings and burns. It is found in sandy places, often on disturbed ground and is an important plant for sand and verge stabilisation. While its natural distribution is from Namqualand to the Eastern Cape, it has been used elsewhere in the world as a stabilising plant and is now a problem species in many parts of the world.

❷ Dorotheanthus bellidiformis
sandvygie

August   September

A striking annual, succulent plant with brilliant red and occasionally white, pink or purple flowers. The flat, lance-shaped, fleshy leaves have fluid-filled, bladder-like cells on the surface and form loose, tufted rosettes. The fruit capsules have five segments that release seeds once wet in the winter rains. It grows in sandy areas from Namaqualand to Riversdale.

❸ Drosanthemum intermedium

August   September

A sparsely branched, low shrublet with slender, creeping stems thickened at the nodes. Its leaves are succulent and covered with glistening papillae (fluid filled, bladder-like cells) on their surfaces. The mauve to magenta flowers are 25 mm wide occuring singly on short stalks. The fruit capsules have 4–6 segments. It occurs in strandveld from Darling to Mossel Bay.

Many vygies have specialised fruiting capsules that only open when moisture is applied (hygrochastic), the expanding (hygroscopic) keels pushing open the valves and thereby only releasing the precious seeds once the ground has received a good soaking. See sequence of capsule opening over a five minute period on adjacent page.

1 Erepsia bracteata

January   April

An erect, sparsely branched shrublet that branches from the base with stems 2–4 mm in diameter. It has succulent leaves about 5 mm in diameter that curve outwards towards their ends. The magenta flowers with yellow centres are produced singly at the end of branches and remain open. The fruits are 6–8 mm in diameter. It grows on rocky sandstone slopes from Clanwilliam to Strand and to Worcester.

2 Jordaaniella dubia
strandvygie

May   September

A mat-forming succulent plant with stems that creep on the ground and root at the nodes. The cylindrical or semi-cylindrical leaves are 25–30 mm long. It produces bright yellow flowers in winter that are 25–30 mm across. The fruit capsules have 10–15 segments. It grows in strandveld vegetation from Elandsbaai to Stilbaai.

3 Lampranthus aestivus

March   October to

An erect, stiffly branched shrublet with erect, pitted, greyish leaves that are 10–15 mm long. The leaves are flattened from the side and widened like the prow of a boat above. It bears numerous white or pink flowers about 25 mm in diameter on flowering stalks that are about 20 mm long. Its discovery on Grootbos was an important range extension for this species which was previously thought to be restricted to the coastal belt between the Cape Peninsula and Kleinmond.

4 Lampranthus caudatus

April   May

A rigid shrublet, with slender, densely leafy branches. The leaves are rough, grey-green, spreading upwards, recurved at the tips and 9–14 mm long. It has 1–3 pink to pale pink flowers about 20 mm in diameter on slender flowering stalks that are 10–20 mm long. This is an Agulhas Plain endemic associated with lowland fynbos vegetation, in quartzitic sand over limestone, ferricrete and sandstone.

① Lamprathus explanatus

    August

A creeping perennial with slender, trailing branches and erect, narrow leaves is in tufts, about 2 mm in diameter. It produces yellow flowers on long flowering stalks and grows in strandveld on sandy flats from Redelinghuis to Cape Peninsula, eastwards as far as Albertinia.

② Lampranthus glomeratus
February   November to

An erect shrublet with slender, sharp pointed leaves that are 12–18 mm long, have prominent dots and are fused at the base. It produces numerous violet or rose-purple flowers that are up to 25 mm in diameter. Its fruits are about 6 mm in diameter. Its discovery on Grootbos provided a range extension for this species, which was previously thought to grow only between the Cape Peninsula and Hermanus.

L. furvus with sickle-shaped leaves, 1–3 magenta to purple flowers in groups and growing on sandstone has also been recorded on Grootbos.

③ Mesembryanthemum crystallinum

November December

A sprawling succulent annual with oval or paddle-shaped leaves that form small rosettes covered with large bladder cells. It bears white or pinkish flowers that are 15–30 mm in diameter. It grows on coastal sands from Namaqualand to the Eastern Cape.

④ Mesembryanthemum canaliculatum

November

(=*Phyllobolus canaliculatus*) A geophyte with tuberous roots and long creeping branches that are softly woody and rooting at the nodes. The leaves have prominent bladder cells. The flowers are 20–30 mm in diameter and the fruits have five locules. It occurs on coastal dunes from the Cape Peninsula to Port Elizabeth.

⑤ Ruschia sarmentosa

July   August

A prostrate shrublet with trailing branches up to 45 cm long and rooting at the nodes. The leaves are triangular in cross-section, curving backwards, slightly rough and about 6 mm in diameter. The flowers are grouped 1–3 in terminal clusters and are reddish with a dark stripe. The fruits have five capsules. It occurs on sandy flats from the Malmesbury to the Cape Flats and eastwards to Grootbos.

48. AIZOACEAE

Vygie or mesemb family

❶ Tetragonia fruticosa
kinkelbossie

  to 1m

August   November

A sprawling shrub with long branches that often trail and creep through other bushes, sometimes completely smothering them. It has oblong leaves with margins rolled under and bears small yellowish flowers that are 3–4 mm in diameter in terminal clusters. The fruits are broadly winged with knobs between the wings. It grows on granite, sandstone and dune sands from Namaqualand to Port Elizabeth.

49. SAPOTACEAE

Sapote family

❷ Sideroxylon inerme
white milkwood

   to 15m

June   December to

A shrubby, dense-crowned tree with dark green leaves that release a milky sap when damaged. The species is adapted to withstand harsh, salt laden winds and is generally found in dune sands near the coast. Depending on environmental conditions, shape and height varies from very short (<1 m) bushes – as can be seen along the De Kelders coastline, to beautiful umbrella shaped trees taller than 10 m. Milkwoods are slow growers and can live for hundreds of years. Each Milkwood is an ecosystem of its own, providing shelter and food for a variety of animals including birds, insects and tree snakes. Their bark is often clothed with a variety of lichens and mosses, while creepers use their trunks to reach the sunlight. The small white flowers produce a strong odour during summer, which attract insects, while their ripe purple berries are sought after by baboons and forest birds. The bark has traditionally been used in infusions to dispel bad dreams or as an astringent. It is the dominant species in the Milkwood thickets on Grootbos and has a natural distribution from the Cape Peninsula up the east coast to the tropics.

50. EBENACEAE

Ebony family

❸ Euclea racemosa
seaguarri

    to 8m

June   December to

A multi-stemmed shrub or single stemmed tree that has leathery, oval leaves that are paler green below and slightly darker above and have rolled under margins. It has characteristic reddish leaf stalks. The small creamy-white flowers are in short spikes about 40 mm long and mature to form round, thinly-fleshed, black fruits. It occurs in coastal dune thickets and forests from Lamberts Bay and Namaqualand to East London.

Myrsine family

❶ Myrsine africana
cape myrtle

May   October to

An erect shrub with small leaves that have finely serrated margins. It has small, pinkish flowers and globular, blue-black fruits. It grows in forests and on forest margins in shady areas from the Cape Peninsula to Port Elizabeth, as well as in tropical Africa and Asia.

52. ERICACEAE

Heath family

The heaths, or ericas, have been known to man since the time of the early Greeks and Romans, and were mentioned in the works of many classical writers. Of the 860 erica species in the world, 760 are found in South Africa and approximately 730 (85%) of these are restricted to the Cape Flora. For sheer diversity the ericas are the most outstanding of the many genera that make up the fynbos. Remarkably, more than 300 of these are found in the Overberg Region and nineteen on Grootbos. The diversity of ericas means that there is at least one species flowering at any time of the year. Almost all ericas and all of those on Grootbos have narrow, folded leaves, described as ericoid. The edges of the leaves are rolled inwards on the lower surface and almost meet in the centre. Many plants in other families (e.g. *Muraltia* and *Metalasia*) have similar looking leaves, but only ericas have leaves that are channelled, with rolled under edges.

❷ Erica canescens

All year

A lax shrublet with small, cup-shaped, hairy pink flowers. This species is restricted to moist sites in coastal areas and lower slopes from Malmesbury to Humansdorp.

❸ Erica cerinthoides
fire heath

All year

This is the best known and most widely distributed member of the Erica genus in southern Africa. It has a persistent rootstock allowing it to survive and resprout following fires, often flowering within a year of burning. If left unburnt it can grow up to 1.8 m tall but will become sterile in the long-term absence of fire. The flowers are large, tubular-inflated, hairy and dark red. It grows on sandy flats and slopes from the Cederberg Mountains to Mpumalanga.

① Erica coccinea

All year

One of the most widespread and variable of the Erica species. It has large, tubular flowers with protruding anthers. It is pollinated by sunbirds. On Grootbos it has an interesting distribution with a yellow-flowering variety growing on limestone and alkaline soils and a red flowering variety growing on the upper acidic sandstone slopes. It is widely distributed from Clanwilliam to George.

② Erica corifolia

All year

An erect, compact shrublet with small pink flowers that are urn-shaped. Characteristically the flowers turn brown at the tips soon after flowering. It is a popular species for flower harvesters on the Agulhas Plain where it can be harvested virtually throughout the year. It is common on sandy flats and middle to upper slopes from Malmesbury to De Hoop.

③ Erica discolor

All year

A dense, resprouting shrub spreading to between 1–2 m in diameter. It has large, tubular pink to dark red flowers that have pale tips. The corolla varies in length from 18–24 mm and the anthers have long awns. It grows usually in drier habitats in sunny positions on coastal flats and lower mountain slopes from Betty's Bay to Humansdorp.

④ Erica glabella

All year

An erect to sprawling shrublet with small, tubular, egg-shaped, pink flowers. The flowers have four protruding anthers and are lightly honey-scented. It grows on sandy flats and lower slopes from the Cape Peninsula to the Breede River Mouth.

⑤ Erica irregularis
gansbaai heath

June   October

An erect, sturdy shrub growing to 1.5 m tall with upright branches covered with pale pink, rounded flowers (*ca* 5 mm long) that are constricted at the mouth, and are borne on long woolly stalks. It is common on Grootbos on alkaline sands and limestone. This species is a local endemic only growing between Stanford and De Kelders , with some 80% of its global population being on Grootbos. In the past this species was heavily harvested for flower export. However, following research into the vulnerability of harvested species on the Agulhas Plain, the harvesting of *Erica irregularis* is no longer permitted.

❶ Erica magnisylvae
grootbos erica

March   May

An erect, non-sprouting shrub with closely packed ericoid leaves and small, white wind-pollinated flowers. This species was first recorded on Grootbos in 1997 and has only ever been recorded on the reserve. The Latin name refers to its discovery on Grootbos, magnus = large and sylva (or silva in classical Latin) = wood, forest; magnisylvae = of the large forest. The localities where it has been recorded start on Swartkransberg and run due west for about 2.5 km. There the species occurs on southern to southwestern slopes mainly in deep brownish grey sand, apparently wind-blown, overlying calcrete deposits which have many sandstone intrusions.

Ericoid leaves

The hard, waxy upper surface of ericoid leaves do not allow transpiration, so the exchange of gases, and therefore loss of moisture, occurs only on the lower surface. Transpiration takes place into the narrow chamber formed by the rolled-under leaf edges. The chamber is protected at the slit-like opening by numerous interlocking hairs. The resultant reduction in the amount of water lost to the atmosphere during transpiration is an important advantage for plants in a climate characterised by long periods of summer drought.

❷ Erica nudiflora

February   June

An erect, compact to sprawling shrublet which is characterised by having hairy leaves and stems but smooth flowers. The flowers are pink with a more or less tubular to egg-shaped corolla 3–5 mm long. Another distinguishing characteristic are the protruding brown stamens. It flowers during the hottest months of the year in late summer and turns the higher slopes of Grootbos bright pink during this time. This species is common and widespread in the south-western Cape and can be found growing on dry, stony slopes from the Cederberg southwards to the Cape Peninsula and eastwards to Bredasdorp.

❸ Erica penicilliformis
salt and pepper

All year

An erect shrublet with urn-shaped corollas, with brown muticous anthers that protrude out of the flower. The Latin name *penicilliformis* is derived from the likeness of its flowers to a pencil or artists brush. It is a popular species for wildflower bouquets. This is a very variable species that grows in different forms and flowers at different times of the year depending on where it occurs. On Grootbos it is a characteristic species of the lower sandstone slopes and flowers from April to June. It is a widespread species with a natural distribution from Clanwilliam to the Tsistikamma Mountains and inland to Oudsthoorn.

❶ Erica pluckenetii subsp. linearis

cats tail erica

An erect, well-branched shrub with long, soft leaves giving it a feathery appearance. The pendulous, inflated, tube-shaped flowers (7–10 mm long) vary from white to red (only the red form is found on Grootbos), and have protruding brown anthers. This sub-species was up until recently categorised as its own species (*Erica lineata*). Recent taxonomic studies have placed it back within the large Erica plukenettii complex. This subspecies is restricted to neutral soils between Gansbaai and Bredasdorp on the Agulhas Plain where it is heavily harvested for the cut flower industry.

❷ Erica pulchella

A very attractive, small shrub (*pulchellus* = beautiful in Latin) with its erect branches covered with bright purplish red flowers. When young these plants are very floriferous, becoming lanky and flowering less as they age. The corolla is 3–4 mm long and is usually urn-shaped, flaring at the mouth. The species occurs from the Cape Peninsula eastwards to Albertinia.

❸ Erica riparia

A low and straggly Erica that is restricted to marshy areas that remain wet throughout the year. Its branches twine around other vegetation. The flowers, which have roundish corolla about 2 mm long, are borne in small clusters and are purplish red and sticky. The anthers protrude well beyond the corolla mouth. Only a few collections have been recorded of this rare species near Gansbaai and one locality at Brandfontein near Cape Agulhas. The discovery of this species on Grootbos on its newly acquired Witvoetskloof property in August 2009 was therefore highly significant.

❹ Erica sessiliflora

green heath

An erect shrub with thick, closely packed leaves and yellowish-green tubular flowers (16–30 mm long). The long tubular flowers are adapted for pollination by sunbirds. Following maturation the flowers form reddish, hard heads of fruit that remain on the plant for many years. This unusual characteristic, together with its yellow-green flowers, makes this species easy to identify. On Grootbos this species grows on neutral to acidic soils, often together with the restio *Elegia thyrsifera*. A widespread species of flats and lower slopes between Piketberg and Humansdorp.

1 Erica vestita

to 90cm

May   August to

A compact shrub with thin, densely packed leaves. It has tubular flowers that vary in colour from dark red through pink to white. On Grootbos the flowers are all bright red. The corolla is between 17–25 mm in length and flares at the mouth with protruding anthers. On Grootbos the species is restricted to sandstone soils and is particularly common on the summit of Gods Window. It is a popular garden species. It occurs in both dry and moist habitats on the lower slopes of mountains between Worcester and George.

> Ericas make use of a symbiotic partnership with fungi in order to absorb moisture. Instead of using root hairs to absorb moisture they use fungi that attach to the roots increasing the area for absorption and in return the Erica provides the fungi with sugars.

A further four species of Erica have been recorded on Grootbos. *Erica axillaris* has small cup-shaped, pale greenish flowers with very large stigma. *Erica hispidula* is a wind pollinated species which is covered with masses of minute (1mm long) pale rosy pink to red flowers that are slightly sticky. *Erica parviflora* has small clusters of pink or red flowers borne in profusion from base to tip on lax branches. It grows next to streams and in seepage areas. *Erica propinqua* has deep pink, urn-shaped flowers that are borne in clusters of three at the ends of branches and is restricted to limestone outcrops on Grootbos.

53. RUBIACEAE

Madder, bedstraw or coffee family

2 Anthospermum aethiopicum
new look

to 2m

January   August to

A compact, leafy shrub with male and female flowers on separate plants. The needle-like leaves occur in whorls of three, tightly packed on the stem. The yellowish flowers are in clusters at the end of branches. A very common species on the lower strandveld flats and slopes on Grootbos. This species acts as a pioneer coloniser after disturbance and is also used as a green filler for fynbos flower bouquets. It occurs on a variety of soils and has a natural distribution from the Bokkeveld Escarpment to the Eastern Cape.

❶ Chironia baccifera

christmas berry,
toothache berry, bitterbos

February — November to

A much-branched shrublet with small, softish, linear leaves about 10 mm long and shiny pink flowers (*ca* 20 mm wide). Bright orange-red berries cover the bushes during summer and autumn. Traditionally the entire plant was used by the Khoi as a purgative and to treat boils. A decoction of the whole plant is taken as a blood purifier to treat acne, sores and boils. Infusions may be used as a remedy for diarrhoea or leprosy. The plant is bitter and said to cause perspiration and sleepiness. It is widespread in sandy and rocky areas in the south-western Cape.

> *Chironia baccifera* (Christmas berry) is an example of a plant that uses buzz pollination. This occurs when carpenter bees wrap themselves tightly around a cluster of anthers and vigorously shake themselves through vibrating their wings for about two seconds. During this process they make a loud buzzing sound before flying off to repeat the process elsewhere. *Chironia baccifera* have poricidal anthers- essentially pollen-filled containers with a tiny aperture at the tip and stigmas which are displaced to one side. Pollen is released through the pore only if the anther is vigorously shaken.

❷ Chironia linoides

January — October to

A shrublet with narrow, erect or spreading leaves. It bears pink flowers with a cylindrical tube 3–5 mm long and produces rounded fruits. It grows on sandy or marshy flats and slopes from Namaqualand to the Cape Peninsula, Bredasdorp and inland to Oudtshoorn.

❸ Chironia tetragona

January — October to

An erect plant with thick leaves up to 25 mm long and of varying width. The leaves grow in pairs along four-angled stems. The sticky, pink flowers have conspicuous yellow stamens. It is a coastal species from the Cape Peninsula to Port Elizabeth.

The spreading, decumbent, *C. decumbens* of coastal flats and vleis, that roots at the nodes and the rare *Chironia stokoei* with acute sepals growing on sandstone slopes at high altitude, are also found on Grootbos.

❹ Sebaea albens

August November

An annual herb with oval leaves that bears 4-petalled, yellow or white flowers with sepals that are rounded on the back and a corolla tube that is shorter than the petals and 2–6 mm long. It grows on damp, sandy coastal flats from Piketberg to Albertinia.

❶ Sebaea aurea

October   December

An erect annual that branches at the top. It has well-spaced pairs of opposite, oval leaves about 15 mm long and clusters of yellow or white four-petalled flowers about 10 mm wide at the top of the plant. It differs from the similar *S. albens* by having sepals that are keeled on the back. It grows on sandy flats and lower slopes from Clanwilliam to Port Elizabeth.

Sebaea minutiflora with white flowers to just 2 mm long are also found on Grootbos, as well as *S. exacoides* with 5-petalled yellow or cream flowers with orange streaks in the throat.

❷ Sebaea micrantha

September   November

An annual with oval leaves that bears 5-petalled, yellow flowers with sepals that are strongly winged. It grows on flats and slopes from Clanwilliam to Port Elizabeth.

❸ Astephanus triflorus
klimop

April   August

A slender, wiry vine with pairs of leaves along spirally twisted stems. The small flowers are cream or pink with maroon bracts. It occurs in coastal or inland thickets where it climbs up shrubs. It occurs naturally over a wide area from Namaqualand to Bredasdorp.

❹ Cynanchum africanum
klimop

June   December

A climber with horizontal runners that are sometimes hairy. The stems and leaves produce a milky sap when damaged. The leaves are opposite, oval-shaped and slightly fleshy. The flowers are brown and sometimes green with twisted petals and are borne in axillary clusters. It is mainly a coastal species growing from Namaqualand to the Cape Peninsula and eastwards to the Eastern Cape.

❺ Cynanchum obtusifolium
monkey rope

All year

A wiry climber with a milky sap that is toxic to livestock. It has oval leaves and small green and white flowers. The elongated, forked fruit pods contain numerous seeds with hairy tufts that are very efficient as parachutes dispersing the released seeds over long distances by wind. It climbs over shrubs and trees in coastal thicket from the Cape Peninsula to KwaZulu-Natal.

❶ Gomphocarpus fruticosus
vleiklapper

April — November to

A soft shrub that branches mainly from the base. It has a milky sap and narrow, opposite leaves that taper gradually towards the base and are several times longer than broad. It bears clusters of nodding, cream-coloured flowers that develop into swollen, egg-shaped fruits with tapering tips. It is distributed throughout southern Africa and elsewhere.

❷ Microloma sagittatum
waxcreeper, bokhorinkies

June — October

A slender, twining herb with small, arrow-shaped leaves 7–35 mm long with margins curved downwards. The tubular, fine-haired pink to red flowers are about 7 mm long with pointed petals. The flowers are clustered together in groups of three to nine and their petals barely open (see box below). The forked fruits give this plant its common name (bokhoring = buck horns). It grows in a variety of drier habitats, from rock outcrops and clay to sandy coastal flats from Namaqualand to the Cape Peninsula and eastwards to Bredasdorp.

Microloma tenuifolium with narrow or thread-like leaves 20–70 mm long and urn-shaped shiny orange to red flowers is also found on Grootbos

The bokhoring *Microloma sagittatum*, a common climber on the reserve, has unusual flowers that remain in a bud-like state with the petals twisted tightly together. The lesser double-collared sunbird is able to thrust its bill into these flowers and extend its tongue to the bottom of the flower to reach the nectar. The pollen becomes attached to the tongue and is only detached inside the next flower through a complex mechanical process. This is the only recorded example in the world of pollen being transferred by birds' tongues.

56. BORAGINACEAE

Forget-me-not family

❸ Lobostemon curvifolius

August — November

An Agulhas Plain endemic with narrow, silver-haired leaves that are generally recurved at the tips. It bears pink to blue flowers that are > 25 mm long and are hairy on the outside. It grows on sandy flats on the Agulhas Plain.

Convolvulus family

❶ Convolvulus capensis
cape bindweed

September   October

A sparsely hairy, climbing perennial with arrow-shaped to deeply lobed leaves that are often toothed. It bears white to pale pink flowers that are 15–35 mm wide with blunt, silky sepals that are 6–10 mm long. This is a widespread species that grows mostly on dry, stony slopes from Namaqualand to the Eastern Cape.

58. SOLANACEAE

The potato family

❷ Lycium afrum
kraal honey thorn

July   November

A thorny shrub to small tree with narrow, grey, leathery leaves in tufts of shoots. It bears beautiful tubular, purple flowers that are 12–20 mm long with petals about a quarter as long as the tube. The stamens are inserted halfway up the tube. A species of dry slopes and flats between Lamberts Bay and Uitenhage.

❸ Solanum africanum
dronkbessie

All year

(=*Solanum quadrangulare*) A scrambling, creeping, semi-succulent shrub with young stems characteristically square in cross-section. It has lance-shaped to oval leaves that are up to 6 cm long, the lower leaves often lobed. It bears terminal clusters of about 30 white, mauve or purple hanging flowers leaves are star-shaped with yellow anthers in the middle forming a cone and about 10 mm in diameter. The berries are purplish black and up to 15 mm in diameter. It is a coastal species that is found in fynbos and thicket from the Cape Peninsula to KwaZulu-Natal.

❹ Solanum linneanum
bitterappel, gifappel

June   December

A prickly shrub with straight thorns, yellow to reddish brown and up to 12 mm long. The leaves are deeply lobed and usually spiny. It bears one to a few mauve to purple flowers in the axils that are 15 mm in diameter. The berries are yellow and 25 mm in diameter. A weedy species, that is common in disturbed areas and has been a problem invader following alien clearing on Grootbos. It has a natural distribution from Worcester and Darling to KwaZulu-Natal.

Solanum guineense with soft leathery leaves to 70 mm long, the glabrous to thinly hairy annual *Solanum nigrum* with toothed leaves and white flowers and the similar *Solanum retroflexum* with deeply serrated leaves and white flowers with purple keels have also been recorded on Grootbos.

❶ Chaenostoma hispidum   to 50cm

(=*Sutera hispida*) An erect or sprawling shrublet covered with rough, gland-tipped hairs. It has coarsely toothed, oval to elliptical leaves and bears pairs of pink to mauve flowers with a yellow throat and a 8–12 mm long funnel-shaped tube at the end of the branches. Only the lower two stamens protrude. It grows on rocky sandstone or limestone outcrops from the Cape Peninsula to Bredasdorp.

❷ Diascia capensis   to 35cm

August October

An erect or sprawling annual herb with deeply lobed leaves. It bears greyish-violet flowers that are 12–23 mm in diameter and have a dark centre and two yellow sacs. The stamens are borne on a yellow swelling and arch downwards. It is pollinated by a specialised group of bees in the genus *Rediviva* that utilise the floral oils secreted by glands contained in the flower spurs. These oil-collecting bees have modified front legs bearing long hairs for mopping up oil! The bees are attracted by the flowers pungent, soapy smell. This is predominantly a coastal species that grows from Piketberg to Stilbaai.

❸ Dischisma ciliatum   to 40cm

August November

basterslakblom

An erect, spreading perennial with narrow, spreading, toothed leaves. It bears long, dense spikes of white flowers. The corolla has four lobes slit in front to resemble a small open, upstanding hand. The calyx lobes are narrow and densely hairy on their margins. It grows on rocky slopes and flats from Lokenberg to Port Elizabeth.

❹ Hebenstretia robusta   to 70cm

August October

A shrublet with erect branches and narrow, spreading, slightly toothed leaves. It bears long spikes of honey-scented flowers that are predominantly white with orange to red markings and has a smooth calyx. It grows on rocky sandstone soils from Namaqualand to the Cape Peninsula and eastwards to the Eastern Cape.

The annuals *Hebenstretia dentata* with ascending branches (also on sandstone) and *Hebenstretia repens* of sandy flats have also been recorded on Grootbos.

❶ Hemimeris sabulosa

  to 50cm — July — October

A sticky-haired annual with square stems and oval, toothed or lobed leaves. It bears yellow flowers that are 7–13 mm long, with two spurs 1.5–3 mm long. It grows on coastal and inland sand and clay soils from Namaqualand to the Eastern Cape.

❷ Jamesbrittenia albomarginata

   to 40cm — All year

A much-branched shrublet covered with gland-tipped hairs. It has small clusters of tiny leaves that are about 3 mm long and often toothed above. It has orange to maroon flowers that are edged with white on long, slender flower stalks about 12–18 mm long. This species grows on limestone hills and coastal dunes from Gansbaai to Stilbaai.

❸ Lyperia tristis

   to 60cm — July — October

An annual herb covered with gland-tipped hairs and with leaves that are sometimes toothed. It bears groups of whitish to yellow or brown flowers that are clove-scented at night, with a slender flower tube 20–29 mm long. It is pollinated by moths and is a widespread species that grows on sandy, gravelly or stony ground from Namibia to the Eastern Cape.

❹ Manulea cheiranthus
vingertjies

 to 30cm — July — November

An annual covered with gland-tipped hairs. It has coarsely toothed leaves and bears racemes of brown to ochre flowers that are 2-lipped and have longitudinally rolled almost thread-like petals and a tube that is 3–5 mm long. It grows on sandy and rocky areas from Malmesbury to Knysna.

Manulea caledonica with large basal leaves reducing in size up the stem and orange to brick red flowers, the hairless *Manulea rubra* of sandy flats near the coast and the densely hairy, sandpapery-textured *Manulea tomentosa* with sparsely-branched stems to 80 cm and orange to brick-red flowers have also been recorded on Grootbos.

❺ Microdon dubius
cat's tail

 to 70cm — May — December

A soft-branched perennial with wand-like stems that becomes woody at the base. It has crowded, narrow hairless leaves 6–18 mm long and bears long spikes of flowers arising singly from dull-coloured bracts. The tubular flowers are pale yellow, often with maroon to brown petals and produce a sweet scent at night, suggesting moth pollination. It grows on flats and slopes from the Gifberg to Caledon.

1 **Nemesia affinis**
leeubekkie, weeskindertjies

August   November

(= *Nemesia versicolor*) An annual herb with elliptical to lance-shaped leaves with toothed margins, the lower stalked and the upper stalkless. It bears heads of white, blue, yellow or sometimes red flowers. Yellow and blue are particularly effective colours at attracting bees. The lower lip having a raised, cream to yellow throat, bearing two velvety swellings and a finger-like nectar-containing, 3–5 mm long spur at the back. The upper petals are oblong in shape. It grows on sandy and granite slopes and flats from southern Namibia to the Eastern Cape.

2 **Nemesia diffusa**

August   October

A short-lived perennial with opposite, lance-shaped, toothed leaves that are 3–5 veined from the base. The flowers are lilac with darker veins, a raised velvety yellow throat, oblong upper lobes and a 2.5 mm long spur. It grows on sandstone slopes from the Cederberg Mountains to Humansdorp.

3 **Nemesia lucida**

August   October

An annual with opposite, oval-shaped, toothed leaves and tiny white flowers with black streaks in lax heads. The flower throat has two velvety swellings, the upper petals are rounded and the spur is short, 0.5–1.5 mm long. It is found mainly after fire and grows on gravel and clay slopes. Its discovery on Grootbos was the first time this species has been recorded on the Agulhas Plain.

The branched annual *Nemesia bicornis* with white to pale lilac flowers with grey veins and four velvety swellings in the throat and the annual *Nemesia gracilis* with opposite, slightly toothed leaves and tiny orange flowers have also been recorded on Grootbos.

4 **Pseudoselago rapunculoides**

February   October to

A completely hairless annual with linear leaves that are sometimes toothed and often have hairy margins. It produces compact heads of white or mauve flowers with orange patches. It grows on sandy flats from the Cape Peninsula to Pearly Beach.

5 **Pseudoselago verbenaceae**

February   September to

A tall, hairless, short-lived perennial with opposite, oblong to lance-shaped, toothed leaves. It produces flat-topped clusters of mauve flowers with orange patches, funnel-shaped tubes and 2-lobed upper lips. It is prolific after fire and grows in seeps and alongside streams from the Hex River Mountains to Agulhas.

❶ Selago canescens

July   September

A densely leafy shrublet with hairy branches. It has leaves that are in tufts, lance-shaped and minutely hairy. It bears flowers in small round mauve heads that form narrow compact panicles. It grows on dry slopes from Bellville to Port Elizabeth.

❷ Selago scabrida

March   October to

A densely leafy shrublet with hairy stems and oblong, tufted leaves. It has white flowers in narrow spikes and grows on rocky slopes between the Cape Peninsula and Swellendam.

Selago aspera with linear, non-tufted leaves, midrib raised beneath and white flowers and the dwarf *S.thomii* with adpressed, linear 2–4 mm long leaves have also been recorded on Grootbos.

❸ Zaluzianskya capensis
verfblommetjie

April   December

A slender, erect annual that is usually hairy. It has narrow, stalkless leaves that are up to 40 mm long. The 25–40 mm long flower tubes contain two large and two small stamens. The flowers are white with a red reverse and are about 50 mm long. They remain tightly closed during the day and open with a strong scent in the evening. It is moth-pollinated and produces a many-seeded capsule. It grows on dune sands and lower slopes from Namaqualand to the Eastern Cape.

❹ Zaluzianskya villosa
drumsticks

June   November

A branched annual with hairs bending backwards and narrow, hairy leaves about 35 mm long. The flowers are white or lilac, often yellow-eyed with a purple reverse, have five deeply notched petals and only two stamens. The flowers are crowded at the end of the branches and have a flower tube that is 10–25 mm long. It is found on sandy flats and lower slopes from Langebaan to Pearly Beach.

❶ Leonotis leonurus
wild dagga

March   May

A fast growing shrub with velvety stems that are woody at the base. The leaves are lance-shaped, rough above, velvety below, with serrated edges. It flowers profusely in autumn with its characteristic bright orange flowers carried in compact clusters in whorls along the flower stalk. Apricot and creamy white flowered forms also occur and are available in the Green Futures nursery. This is an excellent plant for attracting birdlife to your garden as the flowers produce copious nectar, which attracts birds, bees and butterflies. The wild dagga is fast growing and is frost hardy. It should be well watered in summer but does not require much water in the winter months. It is very easy to grow and plants should be cut back at the end of winter. It has traditionally been used as a medicine to treat fevers, headaches, coughs, dysentery and many other conditions. It is also used as a remedy for snake bite and as a charm to keep snakes away. Despite its name, it is only mildly narcotic and has been smoked for the relief of epilepsy. A widespread species that grows in a variety of habitats from Clanwilliam to Gauteng.

❷ Salvia africana-lutea
brown sage, strandsalie

June   December

A much-branched aromatic shrub with densely packed grey, finely hairy leaves. The orange-brown flowers are clustered at the ends of the stems and have a long, hooded upper lip. This is another excellent plant for fynbos gardens. It attracts birds, has unusual rust-orange flowers that fade to reddish brown and later produce the added attraction of saucer-like calyxes once the petals have fallen. Brown sage has traditionally been used as a tea for coughs, colds, bronchitis and female ailments (pour 1 cup of boiling water over a short (70 mm) sprig of leaves, stand for 5 minutes then strain and drink sweetened with honey). The leaves are also used in potpourri as they retain their shape, colour and much of their fragrance, and mix well with other ingredients. It grows naturally on dune sands from Namaqualand to the Cape Peninsula and eastwards to Port Alfred.

> *Salvia africana* flowers contain sweet nectar which acts as an essential food source for sunbirds, particularly when proteas are not flowering. The hinged anthers of this species are triggered by the probing beak of sunbirds in search of nectar at the bottom of the flower. The anthers bend forward and dab pollen on top of the back of the bird's head for transfer to other Salvia flowers.

1 ## Stachys aethiopica
katpisbossie

August   September

An aromatic, straggling, herbaceous plant with toothed, hairy leaves about 20 mm long and 8–12 mm wide on a square stem. It has white to pink hooded flowers about 20 mm long with purple flecks and a large lower lip. It is a widespread species that grows in fynbos and in forests between the Cederberg and Port Elizabeth and further north into tropical Africa.

The prickly, sprawling *Stachys thunbergii* with finely toothed oval-shaped leaves and red to purple flowers is also found on sandstone soils on Grootbos.

61. OROBANCHACEAE

Broomrape family

2 ## Alectra lurida

September   December

A hemiparasitic plant (meaning that it carries out its own photosynthesis but depends on another plant for its water and mineral salts) with minute, slightly toothed leaves and cream-coloured to orange flowers in spikes. It grows on stony slopes and flats from the Cape Peninsula to Knysna.

3 ## Alectra sessiliflora
verfblommetjie

April   November to

A hemiparasitic plant with leaves that are coarsely toothed below and longer than the flower buds. It produces spikes of yellow to orange flowers with unequal stamens and smooth filaments. The vernacular name, *verfblommetjie*, refers to the early use of the rootstock as a source of an orange-yellow dye used for fabric colouring. It grows on damp flats and lower slopes from Gifberg to tropical Africa and Madagascar.

4 ## Harveya capensis
witinkblom

February   November to

A leafless branched or unbranched, slender, parasitic perennial. It bears a loose head of sharply curved, narrow funnel-shaped white flowers that are 25–40 mm long, with a yellow, keyhole-shaped throat and a lobed calyx. The flowers are scented at night. The plant turns black when dried and was used by early settlers in the Cape as a source of writing ink.

❶ Harveya purpurea
persinkblom

September   December

(=*Harveya tubulosa*) A fully parasitic perennial that bears short racemes of fragrant, funnel-shaped pale yellow or white to pink flowers with yellow blotches in the throat that are 25–35 mm long. The calyx is lobed more than halfway. It grows on sandstone slopes from the Cape Peninsula to the Eastern Cape.

Seventy-five percent of all bird-pollinated plants in South Africa occur in the Cape flora, where about 430 species are bird-pollinated. Species dependent on birds for pollination range from bulbs, such as *Haemanthus coccineus*, the bizarre parasitic *Hyobanche sanguineus* (the cat's nails) to the common brown sage, *Salvia africana-lutea*.

❷ Hyobanche sanguinea
snail flower, cat's nails, wolwekos

August   October

A fleshy, leafless parasite that relies entirely on its host for food and water. It has an unbranched stem that bears crowded, velvety red flowers that are 30–50 mm long. The characteristic curved anthers protruding from the flower give it the common name 'cat's nails' (katnaels in Afrikaans). It is pollinated by sunbirds and widespread in sandy places from southern Namibia to Swaziland.

Other species in the family Orobanchaceae that have been recorded on Grootbos are the partly parasitic *Melasma scabrum* with pairs of stalkless, lance-shaped leaves and sweetly scented funnell shaped white or cream flowers with a purple or brownish throat and growing in wetland vegetation and *Orobanche ramosa* with blue-mauve flowers in a spike, in Milkwood thicket.

62. LENTIBULARIACEAE

Bladderwort family

❸ Urticularia bisquamata
bladderwort

January   September to

A delicate annual herb with small, narrow leaves at the base. It bears thin and wiry racemes of 2-lipped, white to lilac flowers with a smooth yellow throat at the base of the lower lip. It grows in marshy, acidic sandstone soils throughout southern Africa.

1 Roella compacta

A sprawling or decumbent shrublet that has coarse leaves with prickly toothed or roughly hairy margins. The flower bracts are toothed above and ciliate below. It has white, or more commonly, pale blue flowers in terminal heads that are 8–10 mm in diameter. It grows on rocky coastal limestone from the Cape Peninsula to De Hoop.

2 Roella incurva

A sturdy, branched shrublet with white-hairy stems and narrow incurved spiny/prickly leaves that are 8 mm long and have a thickened midrib beneath, sometimes with hairs in tufts. The regular white or blue flowers, often with dark blotches on the rim of the petal cup, are 20–30 mm across, the petals are pointed and occur in groups of 1–3 at branch tips. It is common and widespread on sandy lower slopes from Tulbagh to Potberg.

Roella arenaria bears solitary, white or pale blue unmarked flowers.

3 Wahlenbergia androsacea
hare-bell

A tufted annual herb with rough-haired, paddle-shaped leaves with wavy or crisped margins, mostly in a basal tuft. It bears flat-topped panicles of cup-shaped, white to pale blue flowers 5–15 mm in diameter and grows on sandy flats from southern Namibia to tropical Africa.

4 Wahlenbergia longifolia

An erect shrublet with narrow, flat leaves that are often in tufts and sometimes recurved and slightly toothed towards the base. It bears narrow, raceme-like panicles of star-shaped, white or cream flowers 5–8 mm in diameter, with a tube about 1 mm long. It grows on coastal sands and limestone from Hopefield to De Hoop.

5 Wahlenbergia procumbens

A trailing, shortly hairy perennial that forms dense mats and roots at the nodes. It has opposite, elliptic, leaves with leaf margins with rounded projections. The white, blue or mauve flowers are 8–10 mm in diameter and solitary in the axils. It grows in damp, sheltered places from the Koue Bokkeveld to the Cape Peninsula and to the Eastern Cape.

① Wahlenbergia tenella

May   November to

An erect or sprawling shrublet with strongly recurved oval leaves that have a thick margin and sometimes minute teeth below. It has regular white or blue flowers that are 5–8 mm across with narrow, spreading petals clustered in the upper axils or on a flower stalk. It grows on coastal flats and slopes from Mamre to the Eastern Cape.

Also found on Grootbos are *Wahlenbergia cernua,* which is a rough-haired annual herb with elliptical leaves scattered up the stem, *W. paniculata,* which branches from the base with small lance-shaped leaves and white or blue flowers with a white cup and dark ring in the throat and *W. polyantha,* which has tufted leaves with thickened margins and flowers in racemes.

64. LOBELIACEAE

Lobelia family

② Cyphia volubilis
klimop, waterbaroe

August   October

A twining perennial with lance-shaped to deeply lobed and toothed leaves that are about 20 mm long. It bears showy, white to purple star-shaped flowers that are 10–26 mm long and narrow or digitately lobed in the upper leaf axils, 2-lipped and split down the sides with bearded anthers. It is a widespread species, that occurs in many habitats between Clanwilliam and Riversdale, as well as Namaqualand. This species was once a popular and important wild food in the Cape, it is edible and stores water.

③ Lobelia comosa

January   August to

A soft shrublet with rod-like stems branching from the base and hairless or sparsely hairy, lance-shaped, toothed leaves that are 5–10 mm wide. It bears loose or dense racemes of hairless, bright blue flowers 10 mm long on elongate stems. It is restricted to sandy coastal slopes from the Cape Peninsula to Cape Agulhas.

④ Lobelia coronopifolia
wild lobelia

April   October to

A tufted shrublet with somewhat sprawling, short-haired stems branching from the base. It has narrow lance-shaped, deeply toothed or lobed leaves that are 5–10 mm wide, with margins slightly rolled under. It bears one to few large, hairless, dark blue, pink or white flowers that are 15–30 mm long on wiry, green, leafless flowering stalks, 10–28 mm long. It grows from the Gifberg to Kleinriver/Gansbaai Mountains.

① Lobelia cuneifolia

October – December

A sprawling to prostrate perennial with pale blue or white flowers. This species had previously only been collected from Swellendam to Humansdorp and as such its discovery on Grootbos provided a significant range expansion. It grows in shady areas in forests from Grootbos to Humansdorp.

The four other Lobelia species recorded on Grootbos are *L. anceps*, which has flattened, narrowly winged stems and grows in damp places; *L. erinus*, which has flowers with a white centre; *L. linearis*, which is a broom-like shrublet with narrow leaves, and *L. setacea* with thread-like leaves less than 1 mm wide and branched racemes of hairless flowers.

② Monopsis debilis
wild violet

September – December

A sprawling or tufted annual with slender stems and narrowly elliptical, toothed leaves. It bears solitary, almost regular, purple flowers with broad, rounded petals and a darker centre on slender flower stalks in the leaf axils. It grows on damp, sandy slopes and flats from Namaqualand to the Langeberg Mountains and has become an alien invasive species in South Western Australia.

③ Monopsis lutea
yellow lobelia

April – November to

A straggling, bristly perennial herb with sprawling or trailing stems and narrow, toothed leaves that are often orientated along the upper side of thin stems. It bears stalkless, 2-lipped, sulphur-yellow flowers that are clustered in spikes at the branch tips. It grows around wet areas and seeps on Grootbos and has a natural distribution from the Grootwinterhoek Mountains to Humansdorp.

Monopsis simplex, also on Grootbos, has an irregular dark-eyed flower borne on a long stalk.

The name Asteraceae is derived from the type genus *Aster*, while Compositae, an older name, means composite and refers to the characteristic inflorescence, a special type of pseudanthium found in only a few other angiosperm families. With over 1 040 species, the Asteraceae is the most diverse in the Cape flora. On Grootbos alone we have so far identified 104 different Asteraceae species.

❶ Arctotheca prostrata

September November

A sprawling, hairy perennial that roots along the stem and has soft hairy leaves and white-tipped involucral bracts. It bears solitary radiate flowerheads on roughly hairy stalks, with pale to deep yellow rays and a black disc. It grows from the Cape Peninsula to the Eastern Cape.

The annual herb *Arctotheca calendula* has scalloped to deeply divided leaves that are roughly hairy above and white-woolly beneath and grows in dune strandveld vegetation on Grootbos.

❷ Arctotis acaulis
renostergousblom

August October

A tufted perennial with a basal rosette of lance- to lyre-shaped, toothed leaves that are roughly hairy above and grey-felted below. It bears radiate flowerheads with predominantly orange rays on Grootbos (but can be yellow or cream elsewhere), with a black disc. The outer bracts have slender, woolly tips. It grows throughout the southwestern and southern Cape.

❸ Arctotis schlechteri

February October to

A creeping, thinly white-woolly perennial with stems from a diffuse underground system. The leaves are broadly obovate and toothed with revolute margins. It bears solitary white or yellow radiate flowerheads, reddish on the undersides. The fruit has two elongate-undulate cavities. It is endemic to the Agulhas Plain.

❹ Artemesia afra
wildeals, wild wormwood

March May

A softly aromatic shrub with grey-green feathery aromatic leaves. The species (also known as *Umhlonyane* in Zulu) is one of the oldest and best-known of all indigenous medicines in South Africa. It has been used to treat coughs, colds, influenza and is said to relieve menstrual cramps and pain after giving birth. Fresh leaves from this shrub can also be used to treat tooth ache and relieve gum infections. It grows from the Cederberg to Cape Agulhas and northwards to tropical Africa.

❶ Athanasia dentata

January   November

green and gold

A fast-growing, upright, densely leafy shrub. The species name *dentata* means toothed and refers to the serrated leaves. Its flowers are bright golden yellow and carried in showy, flat, honey-scented flowerheads on the ends of the branches. Each one consists of 15–20 rounded 'buttons' clustered tightly together at the end of a branch and each 'button' consists of 30–60 tiny yellow flowers surrounded by short paper-like bracts. Honey bees, solitary bees and butterflies visit the flowerheads, and monkey beetles forage for pollen. The hard, ridged seeds are ripe about six weeks after flowering. It grows from the Cape Peninsula to Port Elizabeth.

❷ Athanasia trifurcata

September   December

klaas louwbos

A shrub with more or less erect, hairless, wedge-shaped grey leaves that are 3–5 toothed at the tips. It bears unbranched clusters of cylindrical, discoid, yellow flowerheads, each containing 50–100 florets. A fast growing species, well adapted as a pioneer plant for landscaping and rehabilitation. It has been found to cause severe liver damage that is manifested principally by photosensitisation. The toxin is unidentified. It grows from Namaqualand to the southern Cape.

Also on Grootbos, *Athanasia quinquedentata* is a densely leafy shrublet to 60 cm with spreading obovate leaves that are spreading to reflexed, often 3–5 toothed.

❸ Berkheya rigida

January   September to

wild thistle

A prickly perennial with alternate, deeply dissected leaves, margins rolled under. It bears clusters of discoid, yellow flowerheads on lateral branches. The leaves, and the bracts below the flowerheads, are stiff and prickly, but the stem does not bear prickles. This is a pioneer species that is characteristic of disturbed sites. It has invaded coastal areas in Australia having been introduced in the ballast of ships. It grows naturally from Langebaan to Riversdale.

❹ Chrysocoma coma-aurea

January   October

bitterbush

A closely leafy shrublet with spreading to recurved, hairless, needle-like leaves that are 3–20 mm long. It bears solitary, discoid, yellow flowerheads that occur at the ends of branches. The flowerheads comprise disc florets that are all alike; there are no petal-like ray florets. There are several rows of green involucral bracts. It is now an invasive species in Western Australia and occurs naturally from Paarl to Caledon.

① **Corymbium africanum**
plampers

A tufted perennial with roughly hairy stems and thread- to strap-like leaves up to 20 cm long with tufted woolly hairs at their base. It bears single flowers grouped together in flat pink to purple or white flowerheads with five roughly hairy, sticky bracts, the inner two longer than the outer. It seldom blooms, except after fire when it is profuse and grows from the Cederberg to Grahamstown.

② **Corymbium glabrum**

A tufted perennial with smooth, broad, leathery, strongly-veined sword-shaped leaves. It has smooth stems that carry loose clusters of discoid, pink or white flowerheads with smooth bracts. It grows on rocky sandstone slopes from the Cederberg to Grahamstown.

③ **Cullumia setosa**
steekhaarbos

A sprawling, prickly, densely leafy shrub that is sometimes cobwebby. It has oval, pungent leaves with tips flexed down and thickened margins bearing one or sometimes two rows of bristles. It bears radiate yellow flowerheads at branch tips. It grows from the Cape Peninsula to Gansbaai and Riviersonderend Mountains.

④ **Cullumia squarrosa**
snake thistle

A robust, prickly shrub with spiny, curved leaves covering the branches up to terminal, solitary yellow flowers. The flowers are cushioned on rings of spine-tipped involucral bracts. It grows only between the Peninsula and Gansbaai and is threatened by coastal developments and alien vegetation invasions.

⑤ **Dimorphotheca nudicaulis**
witmagriet

A perennial herb covered with gland-tipped hairs, with annual stems growing each year from a woody base. It has basal tufts of narrow lance-shaped, usually toothed, leaves with fringed margins. Bears solitary radiate flowerheads on sparsely leafy peduncles, with white rays, purple to copper on underside and a purple disc in the centre. This species is restricted to the sandstone slopes on Grootbos and has a natural distribution range from Namaqualand to George.

The annual *Dimorphotheca pluvialis* has lance-shaped, lobed to toothed leaves.

1 Disparago ericoides
basterslangbos

March   November to

A sparsely cobwebby shrublet with slightly twisted, curved, needle-like leaves that are about 6 mm long. Flowers form dense, rounded short-stalked clusters of flowerheads up to 14 mm in diameter. The sterile pinkish, conspicuous ray florets in 2's are between dry papery bracts, and the disc florets have densely woolly ovaries. The outer involucral bracts are leaf-like, the inner papery. It grows from Piketberg to Riversdale.

The only other Disparago on Grootbos, *D. anomala* grows on coastal sands and limestone.

2 Edmondia sesamoides
sewejaartjie

August   December

A sparsely branched, single-stemmed white-woolly shrublet. The lower leaves are linear and spreading with the edges rolled upwards while those above are short and pressed against the flower stalks. It produces solitary flowerheads that are yellow with involucral bracts papery white, yellow or pink. It forms white fields the first few years after fire and flowering diminishes with time after fire. It is vulnerable to over-harvesting as it is profuse when harvesters have very little else to harvest. It grows on sandstone from the Cederberg to Mossel Bay.

3 Euryops abrotanifolius
lace-leaf euryops, bergharpuisbos

June   December

A densely leafy shrub with slender branches that are leafy in the upper parts, becoming bare lower down. The leaves are closely set, 60–90 mm long, finely divided into needle-like to thread-like lobes and a deep shade of green. A single, large, bright yellow daisy is produced on a long, straight stalk. They are borne in profusion, making quite a show at their peak during winter and spring (June–October), and flowers can still be found in midsummer (December). It is an effective pioneer and is quick to exploit disturbed or open ground. The seeds of this species are dispersed underground by ants. It is an easy to grow fynbos bush that will brighten up the winter garden. It grows on sandstone slopes from northern Cederberg to Riversdale.

4 Felicia amoena

June   October

A softly hairy biennial or perennial with soft-textured, lance-shaped leaves. It bears radiate flowerheads on long flower stalks, with blue or occasionally white rays and a yellow disc. The involucral bracts are in two series. It grows from the Cederberg Mountains to the Eastern Cape.

❶ Felicia tenella   to 25cm

August   November

A sparsely hairy annual with narrow leaves that have coarsely bristly margins. It bears radiate flowerheads that are about 10 mm across with blue, violet or white rays and a yellow disc. They are borne singly on almost leafless unbranched stalks. The involucral bracts are in three or four series. It grows on coastal dunes or near water from the Bokkeveld Mountains to Albertinia.

Felicia aethiopica is a soft shrublet to 60 cm with elliptical to oval leaves that are often flexed downwards. It bears radiate flowerheads on long flowering stalks, with blue rays and a yellow centre.

❷ Gazania pectinata    to 20cm

August   November

A tufted annual with leaves divided into narrow to elliptical lobes, their margins rolled under and white-felted below. It bears radiate flowerheads with orange or yellow rays with dark marks at the base. The involucre is hairless with the inner bracts very long and slender. It can provide colour to any fynbos garden in the spring and once introduced will self-seed. It is a coastal species that occurs naturally from Saldanha Bay to Potberg.

A closer look at the flower of *Gazania pectinata* will show that at the bottom of each petal is a distinct brown marking with a white spot on it. These patterns bear an uncanny resemblance to female monkey beetles. They are thought to serve as decoy females to attract males to pollinate the flowers.

❸ Gerbera crocea
dialstee

  to 40cm

March   September to

A tufted perennial with a rosette of lance-shaped to elliptical leaves that are hairless to sparsely cobwebby beneath, with their margins lightly toothed and rolled under. It bears radiate, white or pink flowerheads, maroon on the reverse on cobwebby, scaly flower stalks. The involucral bracts are hairless to sparsely cobwebby. This species is seldom seen flowering except after fire when it is profuse. It has a natural distribution from the Olifants River Mountains to Bredasdorp and Swartberg.

❹ Gerbera tomentosa
tontelblaarbossie

  to 40cm

October   November

A tufted perennial with a rosette of petiolate, broad, elliptical leaves, up to 20 cm long and 5 cm wide, at ground level. The leaves are yellow-felted below, their margins saw-toothed and rolled under. It bears radiate, white flowerheads that are maroon on the reverse, on scaly flower stalks. The involucral bracts are softly felted and evenly overlapping. Occasional on dry sandstone slopes between the Cape Peninsula and the Great Winterhoek Mountains where it blooms mostly after veld fires.

1 **Gerbera piloselloides**
swarttee

A tufted perennial with a rosette of elliptical leaves tapering towards the base that are softly cobwebby on both surfaces. It bears radiate white, pink, red or yellow flowerheads on naked stalks that are swollen at the tips and grows from the Cape Peninsula to tropical Africa.

2 **Gymnodiscus capillaris**

A tufted, succulent annual with a rosette of lance- to lyre-shaped leaves that are usually lobed below. It bears clusters of small, shortly radiate, yellow flowerheads on branched flowering stems and grows on sandy flats and lower slopes from Namaqualand to Mossel Bay and the western Karoo.

3 **Helichrysum cochleariforme**
gold-and-silver

A rounded, grey-woolly shrublet with spoon-shaped, grey, woolly leaves. It bears a few globular, disciform, flower heads 7 x 8 mm, with cupped, golden brown involucral bracts, the inner ones tipped with white. It grows on coastal sands from Aurora to Gouriqua.

4 **Helichrysum crispum**
hottentots kooigoed

A sprawling perennial with soft, white, silky-woolly leaves that are about 35 mm long and 12 mm wide and clasp the stem. The creamy-white flowerheads have distinctly crisped involucral bracts, are about 5 mm wide and densely clustered at the end of branches. *H. crispum* is used traditionally for heart trouble, for backache and kidney diseases. The Europeans also used it as a remedy for 'heart weakness' in both man and animal. An infusion has a reputation for the treatment of high blood pressure, coronary thrombosis and of bladder conditions. It grows in coastal sands from Bloubergstrand to George.

5 **Helichrysum cymosum**

A straggling, sparsely woolly shrub with narrow elliptical leaves that are white-felted below and sparsely silky above, with margins rolled under. It bears yellow, flat-topped clusters of many cylindrical, disciform or discoid flower heads 3 x 1 mm. A commonly used medicinal

plant for coughs and colds. Smoke from burning leaves is inhaled for pain relief. Leaves are widely used on wounds to prevent infection. A widespread species of damp places from Mamre to Mpumalanga.

① Helichrysum dasyanthum

     to 1m

 September — December

An erect, spreading plant forming large, lax bushes with grey, softly hairy leaves, the margins slightly rolled under. It bears terminal clusters of yellow bell-shaped disciform flowerheads. This species grows on coast and mountain slopes between Clanwilliam and Uniondale.

② Helichrysum foetidum

    to 1m

March — October to

A robust shrub living for two years. It is covered with gland-tipped hairs and has oblong to lance-shaped leaves that are eared at the base and clasping the stem, roughly hairy above and grey-woolly beneath. It bears clusters of flattened-globular, disciform flowerheads 15–25 mm in diameter, with cream to yellowish bracts. The smoke from *H. foetidum* is inhaled by traditional healers to induce a trance and its leaves have astringent qualities, which were traditionally used to draw out infection. It grows on damp slopes from the Cederberg to KwaZulu-Natal.

③ Helichrysum niveum

    to 20cm

February — December to

A low, grey, twiggy shrub with small linear, ericoid leaves with strongly revolute margins. The white or occasionally pink flower heads are discoid and nestled in the leaves. It grows on coastal sands from Saldanha to Stilbaai.

④ Helichrysum patulum
kooigoed

    to 80cm

February — November to

A straggling, grey-woolly shrub with oval, grey leaves with crinkly margins that are narrowed and eared at the base and clasp the stem. It bears clusters of bell-shaped flowerheads with hairless, blunt involucral bracts and grows on sandy flats and slopes from the Cape Peninsula to Mossel Bay.

⑤ Helichrysum retortum

   to 50cm

August — December

A straggling, closely leafy, silvery shrublet. It has overlapping leaves that are spreading or rolled backwards above, silvery silky with tissue paper-like hairs and hooked. It produces solitary, terminal flowerheads that are shiny white and often flushed pink and brown. It is a coastal species that grows from Bloubergstrand to Stilbaai.

Other species of Helichrysum recorded on Grootbos are the grey-woolly annual *H. indicum* with spreading involucral bracts, *H. pandurifolium* with oval, grey-woolly leaves with crinkly margins that are narrowed and eared at the base and clasping the stem and hairless pointed, cream-coloured bracts, *H. spiralepis* with its lower leaves in a rosette and creamy or reddish flowerheads enclosed by leafy bracts, the straggling, thinly woolly *H. tenuiculum* that grows to 1 m, with linear to lance-shaped leaves broadest below, of damp, rocky slopes and *H. teretifolium* with stiffly spreading, needle-like leaves that are hooked at the tips.

❶ Hippia frutescens
rankals

An aromatic, erect or sometimes straggling shrub that is weakly branched with hairy branches bearing crowded, divided leaves up to 60 mm long. It produces discoid flowerheads, each seldom more than 6 mm across, that are grouped in dense or open clusters at the end of the branches. The flowerheads are surrounded by two rows of green bracts with papery edges. It grows mostly in damp places from sea level to 2 000 m, from Piketberg to Uitenhage.

❷ Mairia coriacea
fire daisy

A tufted perennial with a basal rosette of upright, leathery, paddle-shaped leaves that are broadly toothed at the tips and softly hairy when young, but hairless when mature. The plant has a conspicuous tuft of silky hairs at the base of the petiole and bears solitary radiate flowerheads with pink to purple rays and a yellow disc. This species is restricted to rocky sandstone slopes flowering after fire in the extreme southwestern Cape from Rooiels to Potberg.

❸ Metalasia densa
blombos

A large shrub with lance-shaped, oval leaves 2–15 mm long that are twisted, often flexed downwards, and have axillary tufts. It bears clusters of 3–5 flowered, discoid flower heads, with erect or rarely spreading bracts, the inner ones petal-like and white or sometimes brownish, the outer ones papery and sharply pointed. On Grootbos it can be distinguished from the similar *M. muricata* by its broader leaves with blunt tips and its lighter floral bracts. It grows from Namaqualand to the Cape Peninsula and to the Northern Province.

❹ Metalasia muricata
blombos

This species is very similar to *M. densa* and often grows together with it in the strandveld on Grootbos. It can be distinguished from *M. densa* by its typically hooked tips to the leaves and its

brownish bracts with the outer ones thick textured, blunt and faintly keeled. It grows on coastal sand and limestone from Ysterfontein to Transkei. Both *Metalasia muricata* and *M. densa* are widely utilised in the wild flower industry. The close similarity of the two results in them often being harvested together as 'one species' under the common name *blombos*.

The only other Metalasia on Grootbos is *M. brevifolia* which is restricted to the sandstone slopes, is generally a shorter plant to 1m and has shorter densely tufted 5 mm leaves.

① Oncosiphon suffruticosum
stinkkruid

September — December

An aromatic annual herb (the common name stinkkruid translates to 'stink herb') that is much-branched above, with finely twice- or thrice-divided leaves. It bears numerous discoid, yellow flowerheads 5–8 mm in diameter, in flat-topped clusters. This partly forgotten Khoi remedy is still an important medicine in some areas. It is used to bring down fevers, and is also a diuretic. Asthma and pneumonia are treated with infusions of the plants. It grows on sandy flats and slopes often in disturbed areas from Gansbaai to Cape Town and southern Namibia.

② Osteospermum moniliferum
bietou

March — September

(= *Chrysanthemoides monilifera*) A large, fast growing rounded shrub with oval to elliptic toothed leaves. The plant is sparsely woolly on young parts and bears small clusters of yellow radiate flowerheads. The black, fleshy fruits are much loved by birds and this species provides a great option for a fast-growing species in coastal gardens. The *bietou* is easily grown and makes an attractive garden asset and especially useful pioneer shrub for the new garden. It is a rapid grower, requires a sunny, well-drained position and sufficient space. The shrub is very striking during winter, when the bright dense yellow flowers appear. It is naturally a pioneer species that has a limited lifespan (approximately 10 years) but can be effectively used as a mother bush for protecting slower growing tree species in windy areas. The *bietou* fruit was formerly used by the Khoi and San as a food source and to make a tonic for men. Ash from the leaves and stems was used in the making of soap. It occurs naturally on sandstone and dune slopes and flats from Namaqualand to tropical Africa and has become a serious invasive in Australia and New Zealand.

③ Osteospermum rotundifolium

October — December

An erect, rather leggy, sparsely-branched shrub to 2 m. The alternate, sessile, broadly oval-shaped blue-green leaves decrease in size upwards. There are tufts of wool in the axils of the leaves. The yellow flowerheads are in lax heads, with each flower borne on a separate stalk. The stalks are densely clothed with glandular hairs. It grows on sandstone slopes from Kogelberg to Franskraal and Witteberg.

The similar *O. polygaloides* that also grows on Grootbos can be distinguished by its narrower lance-shaped leaves.

❶ **Othonna coronopifolia**
sandbobbejaankool

A semi-succulent shrub with leaves that have a rounded apex and tapering base, often irregularly toothed and usually in tufts on short branches. It produces solitary, yellow flowerheads on long flower stalks. It grows on rocky sandstone slopes along the coast from the Pakhuis Mountains to Gansbaai. Its discovery on Grootbos was the first time it had been recorded eastwards of the Cape Peninsula.

❷ **Othonna quinquedentata**

An erect shrub with several slender, wand-like stems with ascending, leathery, lance-shaped leaves that are often toothed in the upper part. It bears loose clusters of small, radiate, yellow flowerheads. It is most common in the first few years following fire, where it will often forms dense stands that can dominate the post-fire landscape. It grows in rocky places from the Cape Peninsula to the Langkloof.

❸ **Phaenocoma prolifera**
cape strawflower, everlasting

An erect, stiffly-branched shrub with densely woolly stems and scale-like leaves. It is a strong rigid shrub with a unique appearance. Leaves are very small, knob-like. Flower heads, borne terminal on branches, are up to 60 mm in diameter and contain 800 – 1 000 individual flowers with very showy bright pink bracts. The bracts fade to almost white and become worn with age. Its brilliant pink bracts and large flower heads make it easy to spot on many fynbos mountain slopes in the Western Cape. *Phaenocoma* is a monotypic genus (only one species) restricted to the Western Cape. This species is harvested by the flower industry and occurs naturally from Ceres to the Cape Peninsula and to Robertson Pass.

❹ **Polyarrhena reflexa**
wild aster

A straggling, bristly, perennial undershrub with broad-based, recurving leaves that are 10 mm long by 4 mm wide, with barbed edges. The single flowerheads are about 18 mm across, white above and reddish-purple below. It forms a large, dense mat especially in moist places on lower slopes. It occurs from Paarl and the Cape Peninsula to Caledon.

1 **Senecio burchellii**
molteno disease plant

All year

A softly woody shrublet that is usually hairless but sometimes is roughly hairy below. It has narrow leaves that have margins rolled under and are sometimes sparsely toothed, usually with axillary tufts of smaller leaves. It bears loose clusters of radiate yellow flowerheads. This species is toxic causing Molteno disease in cattle in South Africa where it grows throughout the country.

2 **Senecio arniciflorus**
strandhongerblom

August   October

A sprawling, white-woolly shrublet with oblong to lance-shaped leaves that are toothed above and have rolled back margins. It produces a few to several radiate, yellow flowerheads and grows on sandy flats and lower slopes from Mamre to Agulhas.

3 **Senecio elegans**
wild cineraria

March   July to

A soft annual with hairy, lobed and divided leaves that are about 80 mm long. The flowerheads are purple with yellow centres and have one row of involucral bracts. The Khoi traditionally used the plant as a remedy for chest ailments by sucking on small leaves and parts of the stem and swallowing the saliva for tight chests, asthma and coughs. The flowerheads retain their colour when dry and are wonderful in pot pourris. It grows from Nieuwoudtville to Port Elizabeth and also in Namaqualand.

4 **Senecio halimifolius**
tabakbos

January   November to

A sparsely white-cobwebby, greyish shrub with lance-shaped leaves that are coarsely toothed above. It bears dense clusters of yellow radiate flowerheads and is generally found in damp places along seeps from Lamberts Bay to Gansbaai.

5 **Senecio hastifolius**

September   October

An erect, hairless perennial with tuberous roots and variable leaves often purple below and mostly near the base of the plant. The lower leaves are on long stalks, with much smaller, stalkless upper leaves partly enfolding the flowering stem. The flowerheads are purple or yellow with purple or white rays, about 30 mm across. The flowerheads have a single row of loose narrow bracts, alternately papery-edged. It blooms profusely after fire and grows on lower to mid-slopes from the Cederberg to the Cape Peninsula and Elim.

1 Senecio pillansii

A spreading, densely leafy, thinly white-woolly shrublet. It has pungent, revolute-ericoid leaves and radiate yellow flower heads that are solitary on long sparsely scaly stalks. It grows on coastal slopes from the Cape Peninsula to Elim.

2 Senecio purpureus

A tufted perennial covered in gland-tipped hairs and with a basal rosette of lance-shaped, teethed leaves. It bears magenta or white flowerheads crowded in compound corymbs. It is typically found on moist, sandstone slopes, especially after fire and has a natural distribution from the Cape Peninsula to KwaZulu-Natal.

3 Senecio triqueter

A sparsely branched, densely leafy, thinly white-woolly shrub with linear, ericoid leaves that have a pungent odour. The flowerheads are discoid, whitish on slender stalks bearing scale like leaves. It grows on rocky sandstone slopes from the Cape Peninsula to Ladismith and Pearly Beach.

Other Senecio on Grootbos are *Senecio arenarius*, a hairy annual with toothed leaves and yellow flowers with mauve rays on branched flower stalks, *S. erubescens* with a basal rosette of soft, velvety leaves and compact purple flowerheads lacking ray florets on branched flowering stems, *S. lanifer* a glandular-hairy perennial with lobed to toothed leaves and magenta flowers in lax terminal corymbs, *S. littoreus* an erect, hairless annual with yellow flowerheads, *S. mimetes* a thinly woolly perennial to 2.5 m with entire leaves and yellow flowers crowded in small clusters on branched corymbs, *S. paniculatus* a hairless perennial with minutely toothed leaves with rolled back margins and discoid white to yellow flowerheads, the robust, thinly grey-cobwebby annual *S. pterophorus* with yellow flowerheads, the roughly hairy, softly woody *S. pubigerus* with oblong, coarsely toothed leaves and few-rayed flowerheads in white-woolly axillary clusters, the robust *S. rigidus*, which grows to 1.5 m with scabrid stems, the rounded, thinly white-woolly *S. rosmarinifolius* with linear leaves in axillary tufts, the hairy annual, 20 cm high *S. sophioides* with small white calluses on the end of the leaves and the hairless perennial *S. umbellatus* with leaves characterised by their linear to thread-like lobes and minutely toothed margins and yellow flowers with magenta to pink rays.

4 Stoebe capitata

An erect or spreading, sparsely cobwebby shrublet with spreading, twisted, needle-like leaves. It bears dense, globular flowerheads, with mauve to pink or white florets and brown bracts. It grows on sandstone slopes and coastal sands from Piketberg to Grahamstown.

Three other species have been recorded on Grootbos, *S. cinereum* has purplish grouped flowerheads arranged spike-like at branch ends, *S. incana* has brown bracts, longer than the flowers, giving it a spiky appearance and *S. plumosa* has granular, tufted leaves and flowerheads of tapering golden bracts.

1 ## Syncarpha argyropsis
witsewejaartjie

August November

A silver, densely leafy, shrublet with soft, silver-grey paddle-shaped leaves. It bears white discoid flowerheads which are 15–20 mm in diameter, with conspicuous pointed, papery white flowers with maroon markings and yellow centres. It is found on limestone ridges on Grootbos and has a natural distribution along the coast from Rooiels to Plettenberg Bay.

2 ## Syncarpha gnaphaloides
vlaktetee

October December

A white-felted shrublet with slender, almost cylindrical leaves with margins rolled upwards. It bears solitary, cylindrical, fragrant, discoid flowerheads 10 mm in diameter on long stalks. The flowers have reddish-brown bracts that are dry and sharply bent downwards at the tips. It grows on sandstone slopes from the Cape Peninsula to the Outeniqua Mountains.

A third species, *S. canescens,* grows on limestone fynbos on Grootbos with pink to red flowerheads and small elliptic leaves.

3 ## Trichogyne repens
witnaaldebossie

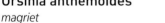

July October

A sprawling, grey and thinly white-hairy ericoid shrublet. It has prostrate main branches that bear short erect flowering branches to 10 cm, terminating in tight rounded clusters of cream coloured flowerheads. It grows on coastal dunes and sandy flats from Vredenburg to Mossel Bay.

4 ## Ursinia anthemoides
magriet

August October

An annual herb with once- or twice-divided leaves that are 20–50 mm long. It bears solitary, radiate yellow to orange flowerheads that are 15–60 mm in diameter on slender flower stalks. Sometimes the rays are darker on the reverse and have a dark central disk. The pappus comprises five scales only. It grows over a large area from Namibia to the Eastern Cape.

❶ Ursinia chrysanthemoides

   to 45cm  August   November

A sprawling or creeping annual or weak perennial, rooting along the stem, with finely twice-divided leaves that are 20–50 mm long. It bears solitary, radiate flowerheads 25–50 mm in diameter on long stalks, with yellow, orange, white or red rays, darker reverse, and a glossy disc. It grows on sandy and gravel slopes and flats from Namaqualand to the Eastern Cape.

❷ Ursinia paleacea
geelmagriet

  to 50cm  August   December

A herbaceous shrublet with finely-lobed leaves that are about 50 mm long. The solitary, yellow flowerheads are borne at the end of slender, bare stems and the ray 'petals' are yellow with dark markings at the base. There are several rows of fairly broad flower bracts with the innermost having conspicuous and characteristic papery tips. It occurs on damp mountain slopes between the Cape Peninsula and Humansdorp.

❸ Ursinia tenuifolia

   to 50cm March   September to

A tufted shrublet with linear, undivided leaves clustered near the base of the plant. The yellow flowerheads are radiate, 15–30 mm in diameter and borne on the ends of long, naked stalks. As is characteristic of the genus Ursinia, the outer bracts are characteristically papery. This species occurs in areas that are seasonally wet from the Cape Peninsula to Albertinia.

Ursinia dentata with shortly divided leaves with finely pointed lobes, solitary radiate flowerheads on elongate wiry stalk, with yellow rays, darker on the reverse and a yellow disc on dry sandstone or limestone, *Ursinia nudicaulis* with leaves crowded below, divided with linear lobes on damp sandstone slopes, *Ursinia punctata* with finely divided leaves, with oblong lobes on damp sandstone slopes also occur on Grootbos.

❹ Vellereophyton dealbatum

to 20cm March   July to

A sprawling, white-woolly annual with inversely lance-shaped leaves. The white discoid flower-heads are crowded in dense, woolly terminal heads with reddish bracts in the centre. This species has become a weedy invader in Western Australia. It grows naturally in damp sites from Namaqualand to Alexandria.

❶ Berzelia lanuginosa
kolkol

A tall shrub with short-stalked, soft-textured needle-like leaves on soft, hanging branches. The small cream flowers are grouped into heads of about 7 mm diameter that resemble dense, round balls of flowers in a branched head. It is one of the most heavily harvested species on the Agulhas Plain, used predominantly as a filler for fynbos bouquets. It grows on sandy flats and slopes in permanently moist sites between Clanwilliam and Bredasdorp.

❷ Staavia radiata
Altydbos

A rounded, twiggy shrub that sprouts from a woody rootstock following fire. It has narrow lance-shaped leaves that are 4–10 mm long and have black dots at their tips (as is characteristic of the family *Bruniaceae*). It bears small pink flowers in heads that are about 5 mm across, surrounded by a whorl of small white bracts. It is a popular flower for fynbos bouquets and grows from Yzerfontein to Gouritsmond.

The only other Bruniaceae recorded on Grootbos is the sprouting, *Bunia laevis*, with 15 mm wide, rounded flowerheads and stiff overlapping grey leaves that is very popular in the local fynbos flower industry.

67. DIPSACACEAE

Scabious family

❸ Scabiosa incisa

A straggling perennial with deeply lobed, hairy leaves. It produces mauve flowerheads that are 20–50 mm wide on long flowering stalks. It grows on coastal sands, and limestone from the Cape Peninsula to the Eastern Cape.

Scabiosa columbaria of the upper rocky slopes on the Reserve has lower paddle-shaped, toothed leaves and upper leaves deeply cut to the midrib into slender lobes.

68. APIACEAE

Carrot family

❹ Centella tridentata

A laxly branched, spreading annual or short lived perennial. It has wedge-shaped, hairy leaves with margins that are 3–5 toothed above. The flower is whitish and arranged in such a way that the four lateral male flowers surround a single central bisexual flower. It grows mostly on coastal flats and lower slopes from Namaqualand to Port Elizabeth.

❶ Anneshorhiza macrocarpa
wilde-anyswortel

  to 1.6m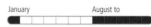
January   August to

A perennial plant with fleshy, fluted roots and leaves that are finely dissected and trailing on long, thin leaf stalks. They are usually dry at flowering time. The flowers are pale yellow. It grows on coastal dunes and in sandy places from Saldanha Bay to East London.

❷ Arctopus echinatus
platdoring, siektetroos

   to 10cm
May   August

A prickly perennial with underground stems and a rosette of spiny, hair-fringed leaves pressed to the ground (4–10 cm long and wide). The male and female flowers are on separate plants with the male flowers pink or white and the female yellow-green and surrounded by 3-spined leafy bracts. This plant was a popular early Cape remedy for numerous diseases and the use of the plant probably had its origin in the Khoi culture. Decoctions, infusions or tinctures of the root (or the white, resinous gum that oozes from it) have been used to treat venereal diseases. The medicine is said to be diuretic, demulcent (soothing) and purgative, and is widely used to treat bladder ailments and skin irritations. The thick root also contains an aromatic balsam. It is a common species of flats and lower slopes from Namaqualand to Uitenhage.

❸ Capnophyllum lutzeyeri

   to 80cm
September   November

A sprawling, annual herb with unisexual white flowers in separate flower clusters on the same plant. It branches from the base with soft finely divided leaves that are 15–60 mm long x 7–25 mm wide dividing into oval leaflets. It has elliptical, smooth fruits with winged margins. This species has only ever been recorded on Grootbos where it was first located in the spring following the 2006 fire on acidic soils. No plants in fynbos burnt the following year. No plants were found in subsequent searches suggesting that it is a short-lived fireweed.

1 Conium chaerophylloides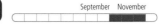

September   November

A robust plant that lives for two years. It has soft, finely divided leaves that become dry at flowering time. The flowers are yellowish green, in flat-topped compound umbels. The fruits are broadly oval, ribbed and square in cross-section. It grows on rocky slopes from Oudsthoorn to the Agulhas Plain and Northern Province.

2 Dasispermum grandicarpum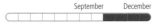

September   December

An erect, annual herb, with herbaceous stems that are not branched at the base and occasionally dichotomously branched higher up. The stems have characteristic conspicuous purple-blotches. The leaves are 40–120 x 25–50 mm and 2-pinnate. The ultimate leaflets are linear-oblong 3–10 x 0.5 mm. It produces fruits greater than 3.9 mm long. The plant was first collected by Heiner Lutzeyer in 2006 following the large fire that swept through Grootbos. It has not been seen subsequently, which suggests that it is an annual that only grows in the year following fire. It has only ever been recorded on Grootbos Nature Reserve.

3 Notobubon capillaceum

February   December to

(= *Peucedanum capillaceum*) A tufted perennial with finely divided leaves in a basal tuft. The leaflets are almost circular in cross-section, erect and lemon scented. The flowers are white to yellow in heads on unbranched long flowering stalks. The fruits are elliptical shaped. It is a species of lower sandstone and limestone slopes from Michell's Pass to the Agulhas Plain and eastwards to Uitenhage.

4 Notobubon ferulaceum
Bergseldery

March   December to

(= *Peucedanum ferulaceum*) A slender perennial with erect stems and finely divided leaves with linear leaflets. It bears small yellowish flowers in compound flower clusters on branched stems and has elliptical fruits that are about 6 mm long. It grows on rocky slopes and sandy flats from Namaqualand to the Eastern Cape.

KEY TO THE SIX MAJOR GROUPS OF GROOTBOS TREES

Adapted from Moll & Scott 1981

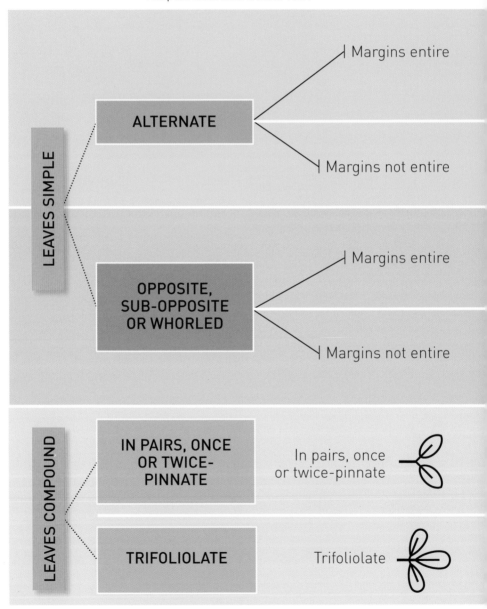

LEAVES SIMPLE

ALTERNATE
— Margins entire
— Margins not entire

OPPOSITE, SUB-OPPOSITE OR WHORLED
— Margins entire
— Margins not entire

LEAVES COMPOUND

IN PAIRS, ONCE OR TWICE-PINNATE — In pairs, once or twice-pinnate

TRIFOLIOLATE — Trifoliolate

GROUP 1
- Apodytes dimidiata
- Diospyros whyteana
- Euclea racemosa
- Kiggelaria africana
- Sideroxylon inerme
- Pterocelastrus tricuspidatus
- Rapanea melanophloeos
- Ocotea bullata   **Pages 272–274**

GROUP 2
- Gymnosporia buxifolia
- Rhoicissus tomentosa
- Grewia occidentalis
- Celtis africana
- Kiggelaria africana
- Myrsine africana
- Ilex mitis   **Pages 274–276**

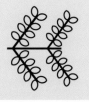

GROUP 3
- Olea capensis *ssp.* capensis
- Olea europea ssp africana
- Olea exasperata
- Chionanthus foveolatus
- Olinia ventosa

Pages 277–278

GROUP 4
- Curtisia dentata
- Cassine peragua   **Pages 278–279**

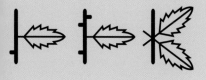

GROUP 5
- Cunonia capensis   **Page 279**

GROUP 6
- Searsia crenata
- Searsia lucida
- Searsia laevigata
- Searsia glauca
- Searsia tomentosa

Pages 279–280

GROUP 1

❶ Apodytes dimidiata
white pear

to 25m | January — November to

A common, dominant canopy species on Grootbos. The bark is whitish, with grey, pale brown and orange coloured patches, persistently smooth with fine transverse ridges. The crown is often draped with bearded lichens. The leaves are 50–80 mm long, oblong-elliptic to narrowly oval-shaped, bluntly pointed or rounded at the tip, with flat or slightly down-curved margins. They are stiffly leathery, dark green and glossy above, pale and dull with a prominent, whitish midrib beneath. The leaf-stalks are pinkish or reddish.

❷ Diospyros whyteana
bladder-nut

to 10m | April June

A small, shade-loving tree that grows in the understorey and margins of forests. It has a slender trunk with smooth to wrinkled, blackish bark that sometimes has white patches. The leaves are 20–50 mm long, elliptic to egg-shaped, pointed, leathery and connected by fine threads when broken. They are deep green and glossy above, pale beneath, hairy while young, becoming smooth except for scattered ginger hairs on margins. The young leaf-stalks are light to reddish-brown and the branchlets zig-zagging.

❸ Euclea racemosa
sea guarri

  to 6m | April June

This is normally a small resprouting thicket or dune strandveld species. However, when protected from fire such as within the Grootbos Milkwood forests, it can become a large single-stemmed tree up to 6 m tall. The leaves are 30–40 mm long, elliptic to egg-shaped, rounded at the tip, with margins rolled backwards. They are thickly leathery, greyish-green, with a prominent, netted venation above and pale beneath. The young twigs are reddish. See page 196 for full description.

④ Kiggelaria africana
wild peach

to 15m

October November

A fast growing canopy species of the Afromontane forests of the reserve.The bark is pale brown and smooth while young, becoming dark brown, flaky and roughly fissured on old trunks. The leaves are 60–140 mm long, elliptic, pointed, with entire or finely wavy margins. They are soft to thinly leathery, dull greyish-green to dark green above, pale grey-velvety to pale green and smooth beneath. The leaves have small warts in the axils of the lateral veins.

⑤ Sideroxylon inerme
white milkwood

to 6m

January April

The dominant species of the Grootbos Milkwood forests, this sturdy species is easily identifiable by its characteristic milky sap released when a leaf is picked. The bark is grey-brown to blackish, rough and square-fissured. The leaves are 50–80 mm long, broadly elliptic to oval-shaped, rounded to shallowly notched at the apex, and with margins curved downwards. They are thickly leathery, dark green and glossy above and pale, with a prominent whitish midrib, beneath. See page 196 for full description.

⑥ Pterocelastrus tricuspidatus
cherrywood

to 5m

May September

A locally common small tree with grey-brown or red-brown to blackish bark, with white patches. The leaves are 50-80 mm long, broadly elliptic to egg-shaped, bluntly pointed to rounded or shallowly notched at the apex, with flat or slightly down-curved margins. They are leathery, deep green and glossy above and pale beneath. The thick, wedge-shaped midrib is prominent but lateral veins faint. The young branchlets are thin and quadrangular, pale green. Fruits are characteristically bright orange and horned. See page 154 for full description.

⑦ Rapanea melanophloeos
cape beech

to 15m

June   October

A dominant tree of the Afromantane forests on Grootbos. It has a straight, cylindrical trunk with whitish-pink bark when young, becoming grey-brown, thickly corky and fissured on old trunks. The leaves are 70–140 mm long, oblong-elliptic and bluntly pointed to rounded or narrowly notched at the tip. The leaves have entire and down-curved margins, are thickly leathery, dark green and dull to somewhat glossy above, pale and dull with a prominent midrib beneath. The tree has characteristic purple leaf-stalks and young branchlets.

⑧ Ocotea bullata
stinkwood

to 20m

February   June

Found only along the perennial stream at Witvoetskloof on Grootbos. This species has conspicuous bulla (pockets) in the axils of the basal veins of the leaves. It has a long, cylindrical trunk. The bark of young stems is grey with white and orange patches becoming dark brown, rough and flaky with age.

GROUP 2

① Gymnosporia buxifolia
common spike-thorn

to 4m

October   December

A spiky bush, common on the margins of Milkwood thicket and forest on the reserve. It has characteristic red-brown or grey-brown spike thorns that are green when young. The bluntly pointed, 40–80 mm long, greyish-green leaves are alternate on long shoots, clustered on short side-shoots. The leaves are narrowly elliptic with entire or serrated margins.

② Rhoicissus tomentosa
common forest grape

to 20m

January   November to

A creeper with 80–120 mm long leaves that are often broader than long, roundish to semi-circular and somewhat 3-lobed, with serrated margins. The leaves are softly leathery, deep green and glossy above, softly red-brown and hairy beneath and strongly 3-veined from the base. The leaves are alternate but the tendrils are opposite.

③ Grewia occidentalis
cross-berry

to 6m

January   September to

An occasional small tree in the afromontane forest, usually growing towards the forest margins. The leaves are 20–60 mm long, oval and bluntly pointed, with the margins serrated all around. The leaves are thinly leathery, deep green to dull dark green and 3-veined from the base.

④ Celtis africana
white stinkwood

to 20m

August   October

A dominant canopy species in the afromontane forests on Grootbos. It is also an occasional species in the Milkwood forests. It is a deciduous species, loosing its leaves in winter and is characterised by beautiful, smooth, almost white, bark. The leaves are 30–70 mm long, oval-shaped, long-tipped and usually pointed, with margins serrated in the upper part only. The leaves are tender, bright green to deep green, strongly 3-veined from the base and somewhat asymmetrical.

275

⑤ Kiggelaria africana
wild peach

October November

A fast growing canopy species of the Afromontane forests of the reserve.The bark is pale brown and smooth while young, becoming dark brown, flaky and roughly fissured on old trunks.The leaves are 60–140 mm long, elliptic, pointed, with entire or finely wavy margins. They are soft to thinly leathery, dull greyish-green to dark green above, pale grey velvety to pale green and smooth beneath. The leaves have small warts in the axils of the lateral veins.

⑥ Myrsine africana
cape myrtle

May   October to

A small shrub that grows in the shade, mostly on forest margins and as an understorey species.It has beautiful shiny leaves with hairy margins that are serrated towards the leaf tip. See page 198 for full description.

⑦ Ilex mitis
African holly

January   March

An occasional forest tree along stream courses and in wet forests such as at Witvoetskloof. It has grey-brown bark with white patches. The crown is rounded and dense. The leaf petioles are pinkish and channelled above.

GROUP 3

❶ Olea europea *ssp.* africana
wild olive

An occasional smallish tree in the Afromontane forests on Grootbos. The trunk is generally gnarled, the bark is dark grey, fissured and very rough on old trunks. The leaves are 40–80 mm long, narrowly lance-shaped, greyish-green, often with a brownish-white undersurface and a prominent midrib beneath. The leaf is sharply pointed and spine tipped (but is not reflexed).

❷ Olea exasperata
dune olive

August   October

A common bush in the dune fynbos and Milkwood thicket margins. It survives fire by coppicing and is typically multi-stemmed. The leaves are 40–70 mm long, narrowly lance-shaped, greyish green and the tips are characteristically bent back (reflexed). The underside is pale green or brown and the midrib is prominent on both surfaces.

❸ Chionanthus foveolatus
fine-leaved ironwood,
common pock ironwood

September   December

A locally frequent small to medium sized tree in the forests on Grootbos. The trunk is slender and grey, often with grey-brown, red-brown or white lichen patches. The leaves are 40–80 mm long, elliptic to narrowly oval-shaped, bluntly pointed or tipped. The leaves are stiffly leathery, dark green and glossy with an impressed midrib and conspicuous pockets in the axils of the veins beneath.

④ Olinia ventosa
hard pear

  to 20m  June   October

A large forest tree that dominates the canopy in the Afromontane forests on Grootbos. The trunk is long and cylindrical, but conical and flutings in old trees. The bark is reddish brown and flaky. The leaves are 40–100 mm long, elliptic to egg-shaped, narrowly tapering towards the stalk, often with wavy margins. They are leathery, deep green and glossy above and pale with a prominent midrib beneath. The leaves and bark smell like almonds when crushed.

⑤ Olea capensis ssp capensis
bastard ironwood, false ironwood

   to 6m March   November to

A small tree occurring in dune fynbos and on the margins of the Milkwood forest. It is multi-stemmed, coppicing from the base following fires. The bark is dark grey with white and black patches and is longitudinally striated. The bark becomes corky and rough on old trunks. The leaves are deep green and dull beneath, entirely smooth, with rolled margins, 40–100 mm long, broadly elliptic and pointed to round at the tips.

GROUP 4

① Curtisia dentata
assegai tree

 to 15m March   November to

A medium to tall tree with a straight, cylindrical trunk that occurs in wet forests (Witvoetskloof) on Grootbos. The bark is brown and fairly smooth to slightly longitudinally striated when young, becoming dark brown to blackish and fissured into small squares on mature trunks. The leaves are 60–120 mm long, broadly elliptic to oval-shaped, pointed, with coarsely serrated margins. The young leaves and stems are golden-rusty and hairy.

② Cassine peragua
bastard saffronwood

January   May

A locally common tree, usually multi-stemmed, growing in dune fynbos, and on the margins of the Milkwood and Afromontane forests on Grootbos. The dark green, leathery leaves are 40–80 mm long, oval-elliptic, bluntly pointed to rounded or shallowly notched at the tip. The leaf margins are serrated and the venation netted. The underside of the leaves is pale green with a dark, netted venation. The leaves often have a black fungal covering and the bark is characteristically orange. See page 154 for full description.

GROUP 5

① Cunonia capensis
red alder, rooiels

February   May

A locally common forest tree, with straight trunk, grey-brown, longitudinally fissured bark, becoming thickly corky and very rough on old trunks. It is confined to wet forest sites such as along the perennial Witvoetskloof river on Grootbos. It has characteristic 'butter-spoon' leaf buds and opposite leaves.

GROUP 6

① Searsia crenata
dune crow-berry

April   May

A much-branched, sprawling shrub with very short, round leaf stalks. The leaflets are sessile, 10–20 mm long, narrowly egg-shaped, rounded at the tip to bluntly pointed. The margins are rolled downwards and serrated in the upper part. The leaves are dark green above and yellow-green with a red-brown midrib beneath.

② Searsia lucida
glossy currant, blinktaaibos

May   August

A locally common, rounded shrub of dune strandveld and forest margins. The leaf-stalks are narrowly winged; the leaflets are sessile, 30–70 mm long and always narrowly notched at the tip. The leaves are deep green and very glossy above, having a varnished appearance. The young stems are sticky. See page 168 for full description.

③ Searsia laevigata
dune taaibos

October   December

A locally common, deciduous shrub on dune strandveld on Grootbos. The leaf stalk is usually winged, leaflets are sessile, egg-shaped, glossy or hairy. Flowers are greenish-yellow and the fruits round and shiny. See page 168 for full description.

④ Searsia glauca
blue kuni-bush

June   September

A locally common, compact shrub growing in dune strandveld and on the edge of the milkwood forests on Grootbos. The leaves are characteristically bluish-green with a glossy, varnished appearance. See page 168 for full description.

⑤ Searsia tomentosa
wild currant

October   December

A shrub or slender small tree in strandveld or on forest margins. It has long, round leaf-stalks. The leaflets are stalked, 20–70 mm long, elliptic to egg-shaped, pointed or rounded and often spine-tipped at the point. The margins are usually coarsely toothed in the upper part, dark green or greyish-green and dull above, white-velvety beneath. The young twigs are reddish.

THE GROOTBOS BIRD LIST

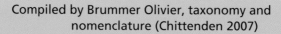

Compiled by Brummer Olivier, taxonomy and
nomenclature (Chittenden 2007)

E = Endemic (25), **NE** = Near Endemic (5) to Southern Africa

#	SPECIES	E / NE	✓
190	Grey-winged Francolin	E	
195	Cape Spurfowl	E	
200	Common Quail		
203	Helmeted Guineafowl		
101	White-backed Duck		
102	Egyptian Goose		
116	Spur-winged Goose		
484	Knysna Woodpecker	E	
488	Olive Woodpecker		
465	Acacia Pied Barbet		
451	African Hoopoe		
446	European Roller		
431	Malachite Kingfisher		
435	Brown-hooded Kingfisher		
429	Giant Kingfisher		
428	Pied Kingfisher		
426	Red-faced Mousebird		
424	Speckled Mousebird		
385	Klaas's Cuckoo		
386	Diderick Cuckoo		
391	Burchell's Coucal		
418	Alpine Swift		
412	African Black Swift		
417	Little Swift		
415	White-rumped Swift		
392	Barn Owl		

#	SPECIES	E / NE	✓
401	Spotted Eagle-Owl		
405	Fiery-necked Nightjar		
349	Speckled Pigeon		
350	African Olive-Pigeon		
355	Laughing Dove		
354	Cape Turtle-Dove		
352	Red-eyed Dove		
356	Namaqua Dove		
231	Denham's Bustard		
208	**Blue Crane**	E	
213	Black Crake		
226	Common Moorhen		
297	Spotted Thick-knee		
255	Crowned Lapwing		
127	Black-shouldered Kite		
126	Yellow-billed Kite		
148	African Fish-Eagle	E	
122	Cape Vulture		
168	**Black Harrier**	E	
155	Rufous-chested Sparrow-hawk		
160	African Goshawk		
152	**Jackal Buzzard**	E	
150	**Forest Buzzard**	E	
149	Steppe Buzzard		
169	African Harrier-Hawk		
131	Verreauxs' Eagle		
140	Martial Eagle		
118	Secretarybird		
181	Rock Kestrel		
8	**Little Grebe**		
62	Grey Heron		
63	Black-headed Heron		
81	Hamerkop		

#	SPECIES	E / NE	✓
94	Hadeda Ibis		
91	Sacred Ibis		
95	African Spoonbill		
89	Marabou Stork		
710	African Paradise-Flycatcher		
541	Fork-tailed Drongo		
742	**Southern Tchagra**	E	
736	**Southern Boubou**	E	
746	**Bokmakierie**	NE	
700	**Cape Batis**	E	
548	Pied Crow		
550	White-necked Raven		
732	Common Fiscal		
534	Banded Martin		
518	Barn Swallow		
523	Pearl-breasted Swallow		
526	Greater Striped Swallow		
529	Rock Martin		
536	Black Saw-wing		
566	**Cape Bulbul**	E	
572	Sombre Greenbul		
661	Cape Grassbird	E	
651	Long-billed Crombec		
796	Cape White-eye		
669	**Grey-backed Cisticola**	NE	
686	**Karoo Prinia**	E	
645	Bar-throated Apalis		
495	**Cape Clapper Lark**	E	
581	Cape Rock-Thrush	E	
582	**Sentinel Rock-Thrush**	E	
577	Olive Thrush		
698	**Fiscal Flycatcher**	E	
689	African Dusky Flycatcher		

#	SPECIES	E / NE	✓
601	Cape Robin-Chat		
614	**Karoo Scrub-Robin**	E	
596	African Stonechat		
769	Red-winged Starling		
768	Black-bellied Starling		
759	**Pied Starling**	E	
757	Common Starling		
760	Wattled Starling		
777	**Orange-breasted Sunbird**	E	
775	Malachite Sunbird		
783	**Southern Double-collared Sunbird**	E	
773	**Cape Sugarbird**	E	
813	**Cape Weaver**	E	
821	Red-billed Quelea		
827	Yellow Bishop		
846	Common Waxbill		
860	Pin-tailed Whydah		
801	House Sparrow		
803	**Cape Sparrow**	NE	
713	Cape Wagtail		
716	African Pipit		
718	Plain-backed Pipit		
872	**Cape Canary**	E	
878	**Yellow Canary**	NE	
877	Brimstone Canary		
885	**Cape Bunting**	NE	

REFERENCES

Bean, A & Johns, A. 2005. *Stellenbosch to Hermanus. South African Wild Flower Guide 5.* Botanical Society of South Africa.

Chittenden, H. 2007. *Roberts Bird Guide.* John Voelcker Book Fund. Cape Town.

Cowling, R.M., Knight, A.T., Privett, S.D.J. & Sharma G. 2009. *Invest in opportunity, not inventory in Hotspots.Conservation Biology* 24(2), 633-635.

Duncan, G.D. & Edwards, T.J. 2007. *Hyacinthaceae. A new pyrophytic Lachenalia species. (Massonieae) from Western Cape, South Africa.* Bothalia 37(1): 31 – 34.

Goldblatt, P. 1989. *The genus Watsonia.* National Botanical Gardens. CTP Book Printers Cape Town.

Goldblatt, P. & Anderson, F. 1986. *The Moraeas of Southern Africa.* Annals of Kirstenbosch Botanic Gardens. Volume 14.

Goldblatt, P. & Manning, J. 2000. *Cape Plants. A conspectus of the Cape Flora of South Africa.* Strelitzia 9. National Botanical Institute. Pretoria.

Goldblatt, P. & Manning, J. 1998. *Gladiolus in Southern Africa.* Fernwood Press. Cape Town.

Jeppe, B. 1989. *Spring and winter flowering bulbs of the Cape.* Oxford University Press. Cape Town.

Kesting, D. 2001. *Wild flowers of the Cape Peninsula. Botanical names: origins and meaning. Flora documentation project.* Friends of the Silvermine Nature Reserve.

Kidd, M.M. 1983. *Cape Peninsula Wildflowers. South African Wild Flower Guide 3.* Botanical Society of South Africa.

Linder, H.P. & Kurzweil, H. 1999. *Orchids of Southern Africa.* AA Balkema Publishers. Netherlands.

Magee, A.R., Van Wyk, B.E., Tilney, P.M. & Downie, S.R. 2009. *A taxonomic revision of Capnophyllum (Apiaceae). South African Journal of Botany.*

Magee, A.R., Van Wyk, B.E., Tilney, P.M. & Downie, S.R. 2010. *A taxonomic revision of the South African endemic genus Dasispermum (Apiaceae, Apioideae), South African Journal of Botany.* 76. 308-323.

Manning, J., Goldblatt, P. & Snijman, D. 2002. *The color encyclopedia of Cape bulbs.* Timber Press. Cambridge.

Manning, J. 2007. *Field guide to Fynbos.* Struik Publishers. Cape Town.

Mergili, M. 2005. *The vegetation of Grootbos Nature Reserve. GIS-based Mapping and Numerical Analysis.* Geographie. Innsbruck.

Mergili, M. & Privett, S.D.J. 2008. *Vegetation and vegetation-environment relationships at Grootbos Nature Reserve, Western Cape, South Africa.* Bothalia. 38,1: 89 – 102.

Moll, E. & Scott, L. 1981. *Trees and shrubs of the Cape Peninsula. An Eco-lab publication.* University of Cape Town.

Mucina, L. & Rutherford, M.C. 2006. *The vegetation of South Africa, Lesotho and Swaziland.* Strelitzia 19. South African Biodiversity Institute. Pretoria.

Mustart, P., Cowling, R.M. & Albertyn, J. 1997. *Southern Overberg. South African Wild Flower Guide 8.* Botanical Society of South Africa.

Oliver, E.G.H., Liltved, W.R. & Pauw, A. 2008. *Pterygodium vermiferum, a new, autonomously self-pollinating, oil-secreting orchid from the Western Cape of South Africa.* South African Journal of Botany.

Pauw, A. & Johnson, S. 1999. *Table Mountain. A natural history.* Fernwood Press. Cape Town.

Schumann, D.S., Kirsten, G. & Oliver, E.G.H. 1992. *Ericas of South Africa.* Fernwood Press.

Schwegler, M. *Medicinal and other uses of Southern Overberg fynbos plants.* Agulhas Biodiversity Initiative.

Palgrave, K.C. 1977. *Trees of Southern Africa.*

Raimondo, D., von Staden, L., Foden, W., Victor, J., Helme, N., Turner, R.C., Kamundi, D. and Manyama, P. 2009 *Red List of South African Plants. Strelitzia 25.* South National Biodiversity Institute, Pretoria.

Rebelo, T. 1995. *Sasol Proteas – A field guide to the Proteas of Southern Africa.* Fernwood Press. In association with the National Botanical Institute. Pretoria.

Van der Walt, J.J.A. *Pelargoniums of Southern Africa.* 1977. Purnell. Cape Town.

Van Wyk, B., Van Oudtshoorn, B. & Gericke, N. 1997. *Medicinal plants of South Africa.* Briza Publications. Pretoria.

Van Wyk, B. & Gericke, N. 2000. *Peoples plants. A guide to useful plants of Southern Africa.* Briza Publications. Pretoria.

Von Breitenbach, F. 1985. *Southern Cape tree guide. Pamphlet 360.* Department of Environment Affairs. Forestry branch. Pretoria.

Whitehouse, C.M. & Fellingham, A.C. 2007. *New species and notes on the genus Cliffortia (Rosaceae).* Bothalia. 37,1: 9-22

www.plantzafrica.com

GLOSSARY

adpressed – lying flat against (usually referring to a leaf or bract)

aril – structure derived from the funicle and partially or wholly covering the seed, usually fleshy or waxy

bract – a leaflike structure associated with a flower

calyx – outer usually leaflike and green circle of parts of a flower

corymbs – a flat topped raceme with flowers all ending at one level

culm – the stem of a grass, restio or similar plant

dichotomous branching – of a stem or vein, splitting into two equal subdivisions

dorsal – denoting a position more toward the back surface than some other object of reference

endemic – Having evolved, that is, arisen in the area being discussed and being confined to it

elaiosomes – a waxy growth/deposit on a seed or fruit, attractive to ants

filaments – stalk of an anther

geophyte – perennial plant with underground storage organs that propagates by means of buds below the soil surface

inflorescence – the arrangement of the flowers on the floral axis

imbricate – overlapping as do the tiles of a roof; may refer to leaves, bracts or perianth segments

internode – portion of stem between two adjacent leaf attachments (nodes)

involucre – the modified leaves just below and to some extent enfolding the flowerhead in proteas, daisies and some other plants

keel – bearing a median longitudinal ridge, as the keel of a boat

lignotuber – persistent, underground woody stem of some perennial plants

moribund – approaching death; about to die

obovate – denoting a prefix reversed or inverted

ovate – oval in shape and attached at the broader end

panicle – a branching raceme

pappus – a ring of fluff, bristles or hairs on daisy seeds between the flower parts and the ovary, often serving as a parachute

peduncle – stalk of plant bearing an inflorescence or solitary flower

perennial – herbaceous plant that persists for several years

perianth – outer sterile parts of a flower, comprising of the calyx and corolla

pubescent – hairy

raceme – stalked flowers arranged up a stem with the oldest at the bottom

rhizomes – horizontal plant stem creeping on or underground, bears roots

scandent – a climber which leans on other plants

sepals – the outer circle of parts of a flower, usually green

sessile – without a stalk, usually a leaf or flower

sheath – tubular, protective structure, as in the lower portion of a grass leaf that clasps the stem

spadix – the central column of flowers in an arum lily

spathe – large leaf- or petal like bract enclosing an entire or partial flower cluster

speciation – is the evolutionary process by which new biological species arise

spur – an outgrowth from a flower, usually to contain nectar or oils

stamen – the stalked boxes which manufacture pollen in a flower

stipules – a pair of usually small leaflike structures on either side of the attachment of a leaf, clearly seen in Pelargonium, but present in many other plants

style – the stalk of a pistil, supporting the stigma in a position appropriate to receive pollen

tepals – the outer parts of a flower, usually 6 in number, in a monocotyledon, in function acting as sepals and petals, but in only one circle

terete – cylindrical or nearly so

terminal – borne at the tip

tunic – bulb or corm covering that is wider than a scale and wrapping entirely around the stem portion in concentric layers, the outer layers often dry

undulate – wavy as in margins

vascular plants – are those plants that have lignified tissues for conducting water, minerals, and photosynthetic products through the plant

INDEX

293